MAKING STORY

Making Story
TWENTY-ONE WRITERS ON HOW THEY PLOT

Aakenbaaken & Kent   New York

akeditor@inbox.com

ISBN: 978-1-938436-08-6

Acknowledgments

This book would not exist without contributions from a lot of people, and I want to thank some of them.

All the writers who shared their plotting methods did so for free and took it very seriously. You have no idea how many improvements and corrections to those pieces some of them called in.

Everett Kaser, who eagle-eyed the manuscript at several stages of development and caught probably 500 mistakes.

Allen Chiu, who came up with the e-book cover even though he was more interested in his prom.

Kimberly Hitchens, Barbara Elliott and Leonard Lopp at Booknook.biz, who oversaw the magical transformation of the text into a tidy, state-of-the-art ebook.

Gar Anthony Haywood, who was my (unknowing) guinea pig, the first author I asked to participate in the project—and who jumped at it, giving me the impetus to move forward.

Munyin Choy-Hallinan, my wife, who originally had the idea of expanding the "Plotting vs. Pantsing" thread on my blog into a book.

You, for deciding to read it. We all hope you get something you need out of it. If you do, please let us know. You can e-mail me at thallinan@gmail.com and I'll pass the word.

So thanks to everyone.

Table of Contents

Introduction

Right now, as you read this, more people are sitting down to write a book than at any time in history.

With the advent of the ebook, many of the barriers to publication have crumbled, and people everywhere are putting words on paper.

But how do you organize those words, those ideas, those people, into a book? Whether it's fiction or nonfiction, how do you transform all that inspiration and hard work into a story?

Writing a book requires dozens of processes, everything from finding the tone for your story to fleshing out characters, establishing an effective point of view, and on and on. Many of these processes come into play as we shape and write our story.

In this book, twenty-one remarkable writers will tell you how they transmute their ideas, characters, settings, and story elements into a plot. How, in other words, they *make story*. I personally admire every writer represented here, and I learned something from every single piece in the book. We all hope you'll find something helpful, too.

It's an amazing thing, considering how different most books are from each other, that every one e millions in print was plotted in one of only two ways.

All writers are either *plotters* or *pantsers*, except for those of us who do a little of both, and even they tend to lean to one side or the other.

A *plotter* is someone who develops the story before beginning to write the narrative. Plotters turn the idea over in their minds, considering possibilities, free-associating, making notes. Then they sit down and begin to outline. Some develop very detailed outlines (James Ellroy has said that some of his outlines are as long as the book he writes from them). Some outline each scene, each motivation, each transition, each "beat," until they have a high-definition road map of their book, complete with its structure and all its characters. Only then do they write the first words in the actual narrative. (This is the approach taken by virtually all screenwriters, and most screenwriters who also write novels are plotters through and through, although one of the writers in this book, Jeffrey Cohen, is an exception.)

Pantsers are writers who find their way through a story by writing it— writing it, essentially, by the seat of their pants. They may begin with no more than an incident and a character or several characters. They may have some initial idea of where the story will lead them: a climax or an "aha" moment that they can't wait to get to. (This form of plotting being what it is, they may never get to it.) I personally just finished writing a book, *The Fame Thief,* that began with an image: 1950s Hollywood at night and a pair of crossed spotlights in the night sky, the spotlight beams held together where they crossed by a pair of handcuffs. That was all I had. (I'm obviously a pantser.) Pantsers grab that basic idea and begin to write, following their imagination and/or their characters into the story.

One approach is definitely *not* intrinsically superior to the other. The one that works best is the one that suits the writer's temperament and mental processes. I defy anyone to look at a good book and tell me whether its writer was a plotter or a pantser. A good book that was exhaustively plotted in advance can feel just as spontaneous and just as unpredictable as a book that was made up on the spur of moment after moment after moment. And a good book that was pulled out of the clouds by someone who had virtually no idea, from one day to the next, where he or she was going, can feel just as tightly structured as the most thoroughly outlined story.

But it's possible sometimes to tell how *bad* books were plotted. To make a dangerous simplification, books that seem to be story-driven— sometimes at the cost of their characters—and a bit mechanical, were probably plotted in advance. And books that wander aimlessly all over the place with no more structure than a bowl of pasta, in which characters self-indulgently reveal much more about themselves than the reader needs (or wants) to know—well, odds are that the writer was a pantser. Good books, though, are indistinguishable.

We live in a time that values spontaneity, and many people probably secretly prefer the somewhat Byronic image of the writer staring pensively out the window as an entire world effortlessly unscrolls itself before him or her, as opposed to the outliner bent over a stack of index cards or a spreadsheet pinned to the wall. But the exact same creative process comes into play whether a story is plotted or pantsed. A world comes into being, people move through it, hopes arise, longings are fulfilled or frustrated. Whichever plotting approach the writer chooses, when the book is finished, he or she has brought something into the world that simply did not exist before; where there was nothing, now there is something.

The greatest privilege of being a writer—an artist of any kind, I suppose—is that day after day we get to be present at the moment of creation. We're allowed every day to make the first footprints in the snow. We get to ransack our lives and ourselves for anything that might work, whether they're fragments of our better angels or the scraps and leftovers of our failures and frustrations, and build a magical realm, motley as a crow's nest, from all of it. We get to experience the moment when a character we create chews through her leash and sets off in her own direction.

And, of course, we get to plot it.

The writers who share their thoughts about making story in this book have gone through all of this, and more. They've ventured, armed with an outline or not, into the unpredictable world of the imagination, and returned with a book under their arm. They've emerged with some tremendous books.

All of us hope you find something here that will be useful to you.

About the Book

At the heart of this book is a series of short pieces about how twenty-one very accomplished writers make story. No two of these pieces are alike.

Each writer's section is kicked off by a pertinent critical quotation about that writer or her work. This is followed by a brief italicized appreciation of that writer (by me) and then the writer's insight into how he or she creates a plot. The plotting essay leads to a short excerpt from a recent book, so you can see what kind of writing results from that author's approach to making story.

Finally, each writer's section concludes with a quick biography and a list of some of his or her works.

As someone who has survived the plotting of 18 novels, I can testify that there's a lot of insight in the pages that follow. Find the ideas that suit you best, and give them a whirl. And let me finish with two pieces of advice.

First, the best plot in the world needs to be written all the way through, from the first sentence to The End, and for most of us that means regular hours in front of the keyboard. Whether the material is coming or not, whether we want to or not, we write. The difference between a writer and a wanna-be writer is simple. A writer is someone who finishes.

Second—and this applies to all elements of a book—when a sentence won't come to you, you have to go to the sentence. If you can't get it perfectly, write the damn thing, move on, and come back and fix it later. The same applies to a scene. A bad scene on paper is better than a perfect scene in your mind.

Write your book. Enjoy the journey.

Brett Battles

"Breakneck pacing, colorful locales and dizzying plot twists."

—*Booklist*

The quote above, while it's a review I'd love to get, leaves out what I think is Brett Battles' greatest strength: an unfailing ability to create fully-formed, life-size characters of both sexes and on all sides of the law. Battles writes full-speed-ahead thrillers—but, like the very best people in the field, for example, Ross Thomas and Thomas Perry, he writes thrillers about people we care about. And that makes all the difference. If all news is local, as they say, then all thrills are more intense and more persuasive when they happen to our friends, and Battles gives us characters who are easy to befriend.

He's also a fearless writer who will always try something new. After making a name for himself with the Jonathan Quinn "Cleaner" novels, he branched out into standalones, another thriller series centered on Logan Harper, and the chilling sort-of-futuristic-but-not-actually (which is what makes it so scary) Project Eden series. As you'll see from the piece below, he's also open to trying something new in the way be plots his books.

Things Changed, So I Changed

I can't tell you how many times I've had or overheard conversations about this topic. I guess that's probably because it's a core, nuts-and-bolts part of the writing process.

It's funny. Writers can be pretty vehement about their particular position. "Writing a detailed outline is the only way to go." "Outline? No way. I just write and let the story tell itself to me."

If you'd asked me a few years ago where I fell, I would have said without hesitation that I was a pantser. In fact, I was probably sitting on the Pantser's Board of Directors. I was the one saying, "I let the story tell itself to me." It worked for me, but that's because I had all the time in the world to write a book.

But then I got my first contract.

Per that contract I had to provide my editor with a synopsis of whatever book I planned on writing. Obviously I didn't have to do this for my first book as it had been written prior to getting a deal. But for the second book? Absolutely.

Still, I considered myself a full-fledged, card-carrying pantser. So when I wrote my proposal for Book 2, I made my synopsis as short and as vague as possible. (Note: I also included the first two or three chapters.) Fine for me, I thought. Lots of room to move around. Thankfully, my editor went for it.

But that's where the problems started. I had a year to write that second book. It sounded like a lot of time, but at that point, in addition to being a novelist, I still had a full-time day job, so as I progressed, I realized that a year wasn't long at all.

The problem with writing without a clear idea of where you're going is that you can write yourself into a corner. And that's pretty much what I ended up doing. The draft that I delivered by my deadline still needed some serious work, and it took another four months before I got the book into shape.

You would have thought I would have learned my lesson from that. But no, I still considered myself a pantser. After all, Book 2 turned out pretty well. So once again, I delivered a two-page synopsis and some sample chapters, and, once again, my editor said, "Go for it."

I'm sure you can guess the result. Once more the process of writing the book (still with the day job) took far too much time. And, like before, the draft I delivered still needed some serious work. (Thankfully, though, not as much as had been required for Book 2.)

So when I set out to write Book 4 of my series, I vowed that I would do things differently.

This would be the first one I would write as a full-time novelist, so I wanted to start off right. But wanting and doing, as we all know, can be two different things. The proposal I gave my editor: 2-page synopsis and sample chaps. The same old song.

This book, though, did go faster. But that was a product of two things. The first, and probably the most influential, was because, as I mentioned, I had no day job interfering with my writing schedule. But the second was that when I hit around page 250, I stopped and took a full week to map out the rest of the book... where I was, where I should be going... from each of my characters' points of view.

(Not really relevant, but here's what I did: I went down to Office Depot and bought those gigantic Post-it notes. Seriously gigantic. We're talking something like three feet by four feet. Each central character got a note, and then, below their name, I listed out, in point form, the story from their POV. I think I ended up having something like eight or nine of these Post-its hanging on my walls. Doing this enabled me to get a handle on where my story was going. When I turned the book in, it was much more finished than my previous books had been. Not perfect, but definitely closer to the finish line.)

I knew that for my next book, I was going to have to do something different. This time I wrote a five-page synopsis along with chapters. That might not seem like a big leap, but it was for me.

Then a funny thing happened. My publisher asked if my fifth book, instead of being another in my Jonathan Quinn series, could be a standalone. This prospect was exciting to me as I was feeling the itch to write a standalone. It wasn't that I was tired of my series, far from it. I just wanted to branch out a little.

When I sat down to figure out the proposal for the standalone, I knew that I was going to have to be more detailed than I'd been in the past. My problem this time was that I had more than one idea, and couldn't figure out which one to present. So I decided, what the hell, let my publisher choose. I wrote a synopsis for three ideas, each of them between 10 and 15 pages in length. These were much more detailed maps than I'd ever produced before. Oh, and I also did sample chapters for all three stories. (I know, I know. Overkill.)

Bantam chose one of the stories, and, in a little over two weeks, I wrote the first 150 pages of the new book. Yes, blazing fast. I'd never written anything so fast. But there was no question that this was a direct result of those more detailed plans.

(Okay, just to make the story accurate and more complete—though, again, not necessarily relevant—at that 150-page mark, I hit a hiccup. I happened to read a novel by a person I respect who had set her story in the same location as I was setting mine. Turns out her plot and the one I was working on were pretty damn close. Too close for me to continue. So what did I do? I wrote another 12-page synopsis, keeping a few of the elements from the story I'd been working on, but really creating something completely new. I started at page zero again on November 4th of that year and had a rough draft just over one month later, on the 7th of December. A month after that, I had a polished draft that was tighter and more complete than any other manuscript I'd ever turned in.)

I was a pantser, but I am no more. That's not to say that I'm an all-out, detail-oriented outliner, either. I'm a kind of a blend, a hybrid if you will. My optimum working process seems to be first creating a 10 to 15-page story map with room to expand and change, and then putting my butt in a chair and writing. The map/outline/synopsis gives me the confidence to plow forward. In fact, I don't think I looked back at my synopsis once while writing that last book. But I knew in my mind that I'd figured it all out, so I knew how far I could stray.

The bottom line is that each writer has a different way of writing. But what I think we need to do is periodically evaluate whether those methods are helping us be our best. This is not some static, forever kind of thing. For a long time writing by the seat of my pants worked well for me. It was really the only way I could do it. But then things changed, so I changed.

And who knows, in the future I may change again.

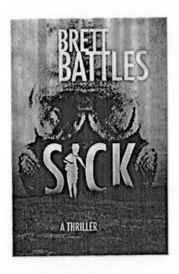

Excerpt

Sick
Project Eden, Book 1

by

Brett Battles

A cry woke him from his sleep.

A young cry. A girl's cry.

Daniel Ash pushed himself up on his elbow. "Josie?"

It was more a question for himself than anything. His daughter's room was down the hall, making it hard for her to hear his sleep-filled voice in the best of circumstances. And if she was crying, not a chance.

He glanced at the other side of the bed, thinking his wife might already be up checking on their daughter. But Ellen was still asleep, her back to him. He'd all but forgotten about the headache she'd had, and the two sleeping pills she'd taken before turning in. Chances were, she wouldn't even open her eyes until after the kids left for school.

Ash rubbed a hand across his face then slipped out of bed.

The old hardwood floor was cool on his feet but not unbearable. He grabbed his T-shirt off the chair in the corner and pulled it on as he walked into the hallway.

A cry again. Definitely coming from his daughter's room.

"Josie, it's okay. I'm coming." This time he raised his voice to make sure she would hear him.

As he passed his son's room, he pulled the door closed so Brandon wouldn't wake, too. Josie's room was at the other end of the hall, closest to the living room. She was the oldest, so she got to pick which room she wanted when they'd moved in. It wasn't any bigger than her brother's but Ash knew she liked the fact that she was as far away from Mom and Dad as possible. Made her feel independent.

Her door was covered with pictures of boy bands and cartoons. She was in that transitional stage between kid and teenager that was both cute and annoying. As he pushed the door open, he expected to find her sitting on her bed, upset about some nightmare she'd had. It wouldn't have been the first time.

"Josie, what's—" His words caught in his mouth.

She wasn't lying in the bed. She was on the floor, the bedspread hanging down just enough to touch her back. Ash rushed over, thinking that she'd fallen and hurt herself. But the moment his hand touched her he knew he was wrong.

She was so hot. Burning up.

He had no idea a person could get that hot.

The most scared he'd ever been before had been when he'd taken Brandon to a boat show in Texas and the boy had wandered off. It took Ash less than a minute to find him again, but he thought nothing would ever top the panic and fear he'd felt then.

Seeing his daughter like that, feeling her skin burning, he realized he'd been wrong. He scooped Josie off the floor and ran into the hallway.

"Ellen!" he yelled. "Ellen, I need you!"

About Brett Battles

Brett Battles is the author of over a dozen novels and several short stories. His second novel, *The Deceived* (part of his Jonathan Quinn series), won the Barry Award for Best Thriller. He is one of the founding members of Killer Year, and is a member of International Thriller Writers. He lives and writes in Los Angeles. More info s available at www.brettbattles.com.

Brett Battles' books in the Jonathan Quinn Series are: *The Cleaner*, *The Deceived*, *Shadow of Betrayal*, *The Silenced*, *Becoming Quinn* and *The Destroyed*. The Project Eden Thrillers are *Sick*, *Exit 9*, and *Pale Horse*. The Logan Harper Thrillers are *Little Girl Gone* and *Every Precious Thing*. His standalones are *The Pull of Gravity* and *No Return*. *Here Comes Mr. Trouble* was written for young readers.

Cara Black

"Wry, complex, sophisticated, intensely Parisian.... One of the very best heroines in crime fiction today."

—Lee Child

As the quotation above suggests, Cara Black's Aimée Leduc is a three-hundred-sixty degree, three-dimensional character: intriguing, solid, and lifelike (in the best literary way, which is to say a little better than lifelike), and with enviable staying power. She's appeared in twelve bestselling and critically acclaimed novels thus far, with Murder in the Lanterne Rouge *the most recent, and neither Cara nor Aimée shows any sign of slowing down.*

One indelible indication that Black knows her Paris and her Parisians is that some of the books have been translated into French and that she received, in 2011, the Medaille de la Ville de Paris *for service to French culture.*

It's often said of detective fiction that it's classless, in that a detective can talk to anyone of any station. Cara adds to that vertical exploration of class a geographic exploration of the City of Light as Aimée, aboard her pink Vespa, solves a crime in neighborhood after neighborhood: the Marais, Belleville, Passy, Montmartre, the Ile Saint-Louis, Clichy. A great character in one of the world's great cities, in books with plots that I can only envy. This is an exceptional series, and Cara Black is the real deal.

Plotting and Playdough

Let me preface this by revealing I was a preschool teacher in my former life. So with me plotting resembles making playdough—I assemble the ingredients then get all tactile, hands on and work with a lump of ideas. Often it involves arranging scribbled-on restaurant napkins, Metro tickets, putting up photos, maps and diagrams on the wall. Messy and sloppy some might say; or among four-year olds we'd call it creative engagement.

That said, when I began plotting my next book—in this case *Murder at the Lanterne Rouge*—out came the colored markers and Post-its and roll of butcher paper. Butcher paper helps me timeline the sequence, action and pacing. I can't outline for the life of me, and dearly wish I could, but I spread and tape the butcher paper over a wall, draw columns and label each column as a day of the week. Each character had a different colored post-it so in my pre-warm-up to butcher paper, I'd jotted words, phrases, a specific Paris street corner on each color that I felt related either to a character or to anything that was said or thought by them.

I'd come up with the location in Paris, the northern edge of the Marais, and knew the story would take place in an area that intrigued me. My stories are generated by place, by a part of Paris, who inhabits this place, the ambiance and why my detective, Aimée Leduc, would go there and get involved. Aimée's partner René had fallen head over his heels for a young Chinese woman but Aimée's suspicious and worried for him. That set me off. Now I began to figure out how the story would play out in this historic *quartier* of Paris. I didn't yet know how this would weave together but I let it simmer.

Then I tacked a map of the streets, a diagram of the narrow small Chinatown centered there, and wrote in landmarks—i.e., the tofu shop, the 14th century building with the Pho noodle resto, the plaque to a fallen Resistance member, and charted out the shops, the bus stops, Metro exits which I know my characters would be using. So I spatially and visually re-created what I learned researching and discovering in Paris previously on several trips.

For several years a few nuggets had swirled in my mind for a story. Now I went through my notes and found the nuggets that now sparked together and seemed to form a story: a line quoted to me by an agent in the domestic intelligence branch one day—"No one dies in Chinatown"— the interview with a graduate of an engineering *Grand École* who filled me in on fiber optics and the 14th century Templar tower and wall remnants I discovered when I got lost one day.

Now I filled in the diagram marking where the characters lived, the victim's great aunt's apartment, the shop where the girl worked. Then I pulled back and tacked on the villain, who deserved his own section of butcher paper—the villain orchestrates the plot, sets the story in motion because of his actions. I timelined the murder—all would be off the page but I needed to know in the columns day by day what he'd be doing to thwart the investigation. Then the story, like playdough, clung together.

Excerpt

Murder at the Lanterne Rouge

by

Cara Black

Paris January 1998
Friday Evening

Too small for a bomb, Aimée Leduc thought, nudging with her high-heeled toe at the tiny red box on the cold landing outside Leduc Detective's office. No card. Curious, she picked up the red gift-wrapped box, sniffed. Nothing floral. A secret admirer?

The timed hallway light clicked off, plunging the landing into darkness. She shivered, closed the frosted glass door behind her, and hit the light switch. The chandelier's crystal drops caught the light and reflected in the old patinated mirror over the fireplace.

For once the high-ceilinged nineteenth-century office was warm, too warm. The new boiler had gone into overdrive. Her nose ran at the switch from the chill January evening to a toasty, warm office. She set down her shopping bags - January was the season of *soldes*, the big sales. She'd blown her budget.

Et alors, yogurt and carrots at her desk for the next week.

She slung her coat over the chair and noticed a chip on her rouge-noir-lacquered pinkie. *Zut*. She'd have to spring for a manicure.

The office phone trilled startling her.

"Tell me you found Meizi's birthday present, Aimée," came the breathless voice of René, her business partner at Leduc Detective. "The damned jeweler screwed up the delivery."

"Small red box? You mean it's not for me?" she joked. She shook the box and heard a rattle. Maybe those jade earrings she'd seen him looking at. "You're serious about Meizi? I mean that kind of serious?"

"One day you'll meet your soul mate, too, Aimée."

Soul mate? He'd known Meizi what, two months? But Aimée bit her tongue. So unlike René to rush into something. A surge of protectiveness hit her. She ought to check this girl out, see what she could learn from a quick computer background search. Could be a little ticking bomb, all right.

About Cara Black

Cara Black writes the bestselling and award nominated Aimée Leduc mystery novels featuring a female Paris-based private investigator. Black is included in *Great Women Mystery Writers* by Elizabeth Lindsay, 2nd edition UK. Her first novel, *Murder in the Marais*, was nominated for an Anthony and Macavity Award for best first novel. The third novel in the series, *Murder in the Sentier*, was nominated for an Anthony Award as Best Novel. *Murder in the Rue de Paradis*, the eighth in her series, was a Washington Post Best Fiction pick, and *Murder in the Latin Quarter* was shortlisted for Best Novel by the Northern California Independent

Bookseller Association. Her books have been translated into French, Italian, Japanese, Hebrew, Spanish, UK editions and Norwegian.

Black is a San Francisco Library Laureate and member of the Marais Historic Society and *Histories du Vie 10th arrondissement* in Paris. In June she received the *Medaille de la Ville de Paris* at the *Hotel de Ville* in Paris for service to French culture. Black lives in San Francisco with her husband — a bookseller — and their son.

In addition to the titles mentioned above, the Aimée Leduc Investigations are: *Murder in Belleville, Murder in the Bastille, Murder in Clichy, Murder in Montmartre, Murder on the Ile Saint-Louis, Murder in the Palais Royal,* and *Murder in Passy.*

Lisa Brackmann

"Lisa Brackmann's first novel gets off to a fast start and never lets up…be prepared for a wild ride."

—*The New York Times*

Does it ever. Rock Paper Tiger, *the book described above, was probably the best book I read last year by a writer who was previously unknown to me. It was a ripping yarn and much more: It was intelligent, thoughtful, spiky, revelatory about modern-day China, and written in prose as pointed as barbed wire. I ate it up.*

Lisa Brackmann proves the first book was no fluke with Getaway, *her second eminently thrilling thriller—this one set in Mexico. What Brackmann does, well enough to conduct a master class, is to create female-centered hair-raisers that never, ever degenerate into the old female-in-peril trope. Although her protagonists are relatively ordinary people—not professional hitwomen on holiday or female soldiers of fortune taking a break from mopping-up operations in some banana republic, they've got the bone, sinew, brains, and guts we all like to think we'd have in those situations. Although we probably wouldn't.*

Bowling Ball, Chain Saw, and Flaming Torch

Whenever anyone asks me how I write a book, how I construct a story, the first thing I always want to say is, "Kids! Don't try this at home!" Because I have likened my process as trying to juggle a bowling ball, a chain saw and a flaming torch. It gets messy.

Also, if you're a writer who doesn't want to write the same thing over and over, who wants to push herself, to do something different – then you're never going to find one process that you can duplicate with assembly-line proficiency from book to book.

However, after selling three books, and especially as I am starting to think about Book #4, there are some things about my own processes that I've learned.

First, yes, I am a pantser.

I really wish that I weren't at times. I wish that I could create a cast of characters, a set of problems, and whatever drivers I needed to come up with a story before I sat down to write it.

My problem is that I tend to develop characters through a weird process that I can only describe as spying and eavesdropping. I know that these fictional people are projections from my own brain, but I usually only get to know them gradually, by watching them as I would any stranger, and seeing what they do and how they interact with other fictional projections from my head and whatever strange situation I've created for them to deal with.

Which brings me to one of my main drivers of story—setting.

Generally, I like to use a place that I'm familiar with and bring it to life. In a way I'm duplicating my own experiences as a traveler—journeying with exposed nerve-endings, taking in every little detail of my surroundings, letting that sensory overload drive out my daily concerns and ordinary worries.

For my first book, *Rock Paper Tiger*, setting was a primary consideration. After writing a bunch of things for fun over the years, work that I knew wasn't all that salable, I had finally decided that I needed to get serious if I wanted to be a professional author, and write something that I had a chance of selling.

I asked myself, what could I write about that was commercial? That was interesting? That hadn't been written about all that much before?

China, I decided.

I'd been traveling to China for almost thirty years. I hadn't read much fiction by Western authors dealing with contemporary China. Most of what I'd seen was period stuff. Nothing that portrayed the rapidly modernizing cities I'd come to know in my recent visits.

So that was my blatant commercial consideration. But what to write about?

Generally I look around for an issue that I'm passionate about. Which for me, generally means something that really pisses me off.

For *Rock Paper Tiger*, it was the Iraq War and more broadly, the War on Terror, and what this had done to the US, to our economy, our Constitution and our foundation of the rule of law.

Except I needed it to be set in China. And I was also interested in the contemporary art scene there, and thought that this might be a cool element to use.

This is where the juggling the bowling ball, chainsaw, and flaming torch metaphor comes into play: how to make these things work and play well together.

The nexus for this book came down to the main character, Ellie McEnroe/Cooper, an accidental Iraq War vet living in Beijing with a Chinese artist boyfriend. I didn't know who Ellie was when I started writing, but her voice asserted itself almost immediately, and her background, her story, followed.

The rest of it was a lot of trial and error and writing and rewriting and learning how to take all of these elements and construct a story with tension and urgency that makes you turn the pages.

Oh, and a unifying theme. This book was largely about the consequences of unrestrained authority: it's irrational, it's arbitrary, and there's no way you can trust it to do the right and just thing. I didn't exactly know this was the theme when I started writing, but it quickly emerged.

My second book went a little differently. For that one, I again started with a location – Puerto Vallarta, because it was a place I knew pretty well and thought would lend itself to a suspense novel. I'd decided I wanted to do something a little noir, which in my definition meant, "A woman/man in trouble meets a man/woman who is trouble, and things go very, very wrong." I had a sort of vision of an American woman, a tourist, sitting on the beach. Michelle was troubled and unhappy, though I didn't know why. She meets a good-looking man on the beach, and in a moment of lust fueled by a few too many margaritas, invites him back to her hotel room. And yes, things go very, very wrong.

The whole chapter pretty much came to me in a piece. It had a nice, dramatic ending. And then I had to figure out what the book was about.

Basically, I looked at Puerto Vallarta and thought, what kind of trouble could Michelle find there? I decided on sketchy expats. The drug trade. A big piece of it came to me when I was trying to figure out the background of one of the main characters. He was a pilot, I knew. In a nearly random bit of Googling, I found stories about how a jet loaded with cocaine had also been used on rendition flights in and out of Guantanamo, and a whole fleet of Gulfstreams owned by a CIA front company had been bought by representatives of the Sinaloa Cartel. Really!

This kind of weird, real-life linkage of what would seem to be two disparate elements is the sort of material that I love to use to build stories. So a large element of how I plot is based on research. Some of the time I know what I'm looking for. Other times, I don't. Generally it's the latter, more serendipitous elements that really generate plot for me.

Both *Rock Paper Tiger* and *Getaway* involved pretty steep learning curves for me on some of the technical aspects of writing suspense fiction. Mainly, how to maintain momentum and tension throughout. This doesn't mean that every page has to be slam-bam full of action. It does mean that this sort of fiction works best, in my opinion, when the narrative thread is pulled tight. Pacing is vital, and tension can come from a lot of different things. A subtle sense of dread. Carefully placed humor. What's important is to pull your reader along, to know when to relax a little before stepping on the throttle again, to end each chapter with a forward that makes your reader want to keep turning the page.

So, to sum up, here are my building blocks of plot: Character. Location. Issues plus passion. Some sort of stakes that lead to danger. Mix well, till on the verge of combusting.

Excerpt

Getaway

by

Lisa Brackmann

Lawyer. How did you say "lawyer"? The only word Michelle could come up with was *albóndigas*, and that, she was fairly sure, meant "meatballs."

Sitting in the back of the squad car seemed so unreal that she couldn't process it. The seat smelled like beer-scented puke. The policeman had cuffed her, hands behind her back and tight enough to hurt. Taken her luggage out of the taxi and thrown it next to her. Was he even a real policeman? He looked like one, she thought--a big man with a big belly and a mustache and aviator sunglasses. His uniform looked real. The squad car looked credible too. Now and again the radio squawked and broadcast chatter.

"*¿Dónde vamos?*" she managed.

"A la cárcel."

"What?"

"Jail." The policeman barked out a laugh. "*Tienes drogas,* go to jail."

"Drugs? I don't have any drugs."

He shrugged fractionally, shoulders tense, hands gripping the wheel.

A setup, she thought, it was some kind of setup. A con, a way to extort money. "Look," she said. "This is a misunderstanding. Can't we work this out?"

As soon as she said it, she knew she'd made a mistake.

"What do you think, lady? You want to give me something?"

"No, I, just..."

"Money, maybe? Something else?" He laughed again, all the while staring straight ahead.

"It's a misunderstanding," she repeated. "I'm not trying to insult you."

"You want to give me something, you want to stop right here?"

The squad car slowed.

On one side of the road, there were cinder block buildings: apartments mostly, a few downtrodden businesses, peeling hand-painted signs, rusting cars, broken-down fences. On the other a steep hill, dirt roads, shacks interspersed among browning vines and palms.

"No," she said. "No."

The car sped up again.

About Lisa Brackmann

Lisa Brackmann's debut novel, *Rock Paper Tiger*, set on the fringes of the Chinese art world, made several "Best of 2010" lists, including Amazon's Top 100 Novels and Top 10 Mystery/Thrillers. Her second novel is *Getaway*, a thriller set in Mexico, an Amazon Best Novel of the Month and an ALA Summer Reading Pick. She has lived and traveled extensively in China, the setting of her third novel, *Hour of the Rat*, publishing in 2013. Lisa can be reached at her website, http://www.lisabrackmann.com and on Facebook at http://www.facebook.com/lisabrackmannauthor. You can follow her on Twitter at http://twitter.com/otherlisa

Rachel Brady

"PI Richard Cole puts Emily Locke on a case that gives her a real workout in Brady's well-crafted second mystery to feature the 33-year-old single mom (after 2009's *Final Approach*). Brady's wry look at fashionista spa life and the spirited, down-to-earth Emily mark this as a series to watch."

—*Publishers Weekly*, on *Dead Lift*

Rachel Brady comes to writing mysteries from a background in biomedical engineering and she brings to her new career intelligence, a quick wit, and an engineer's precision in plotting.

A plot is, of course, a machine. It's the engine that moves the book forward and it's also the infrastructure that gives it shape. To mix metaphors for a moment, if a book is a Christmas tree, the plot is the tree itself, the form that supports the ornaments of setting and local color and wit and good writing. In the best books (from my personal perspective) the plot arises directly from the characters, which is why I don't list characters among the ornaments. Writing a good mystery involves not only creating a dependable, sturdy, and unfailing machine in your plot but also keeping all the actual machinery—the gears and wheels and mainsprings—completely out of sight. Rachel Brady's books do all of the above. The end result is tidy and effective in the extreme, even if (as she says) the process can be a bit messy.

Messily in the Middle: Getting Comfortable in My Writing Skin

Some writers are "pantsers" who write by the seat of their pants, laying the story down as the ideas come. Others, the plotters and outliners, think the whole story out ahead of time. I'm a pantser with outlining tendencies, so I fall messily in the middle.

My first novel, *Final Approach*, came to me in key scenes. Certain parts of that story played in my mind like a movie and, since I saw them so vividly, I wrote them first. This meant that I had a few important scenes from the beginning, middle, and end of the novel but nothing to link them. My struggle was forming the "bridges" between these scenes. Instead of writing from A to Z, it was more like writing from D to H and then L to Q. This strategy nearly drove me mad. I promised myself that if I ever wrote another book, I would write it linearly, from A to Z, no messing around. I was finished with bridges. Burn the bridges.

The random-scenes technique had two perks:

1. There was no excuse for not writing. If I didn't know what came next, I would skip ahead, way ahead, to something I knew would happen eventually. Sure, there would be extensive revisions later, but in the moment, words were going onto the page.

2. Each chapter existed as a separate Word document on my machine. When I was finally finished with a rough draft, I pasted forty separate Word documents together in the right order and watched a manuscript build before my eyes. That was enormously exciting.

While *Final Approach* was being offered for publication, I started working on a new book, the linear, A to Z one. I was a third of the way through a rough draft when *Final Approach* sold, and eventually my editor and I turned our attention to Book 2. She asked for a synopsis first, an overview of the whole book, including its ending, so she could flag any major issues before I wandered off into the weeds. This requirement paralyzed me for a long time. How could I send a summary of the book? I had no idea how the story would unfold. I knew how it would end, but not how to get there.

I e-mailed a good writing friend. "Fake it," came his reply. "Make something up, and if it changes when you actually write it, say you came up with something even better."

Ultimately, I did fake it. But even faking a path took weeks. I made way more revisions than a three-page summary should require. I tried working on it narrative-style and I tried outlining it. In fact, at the time, I was determined to reform as an Outliner. But deep down I knew that if I waited for the whole book to reveal itself to me, so that I could summarize it in outline form, I would wait a very long time. Have you heard the advice about driving in fog? Not to overdrive your headlights? In my writing, the headlights only stretch a few scenes ahead. That's as far as I can outline. I cannot see the end of the road, and I'm envious of writers who can.

I ended up writing that novel, *Dead Lift*, linearly and liked that approach well enough. It was easier to keep the chronology of the story straight, and I did less hand-waving to get characters where I needed them to be. Events unfolded organically with this method. But there were drawbacks:

1. When I got stuck, I stopped writing. Sometimes it took weeks or months for me to figure out the next scene.

2. The manuscript existed as a single file on my computer and I developed an annoying preoccupation with its total word count. Now I'm a compulsive word count checker. I wish they made a patch for this.

When I began to think about Book 3, currently in revision, I explored its premise in a series of roughly sketched scenes during National Novel Writing Month (NaNoWriMo). Participating in NaNoWriMo was an attempt to shake up my writing routine. It worked.

That story was my foray into multiple viewpoints. It presented new challenges, both in the story and in its synopsis. I wasn't sure how to capture parallel story lines in summary form and, as usual, I didn't know how the story would unfold. Once again, I found myself sweating it out in Synopsis Hell. I also suspected that a linear, A to Z, approach wouldn't serve that novel well. In some ways, writing the third book was like creating two novellas with a plan to weave their chapters together later in a way that made sense. The thought of trying something so new and radical frightened me.

But by the third novel, I was okay with discomfort. For years, I'd read writing books and listened to authors at writers' conferences and then rushed to the keyboard to implement their processes. Now I've decided that this is like trying to squeeze into someone else's shoes. What fits another person might give me blisters. Better to break in my own shoes, I think. My process will probably always vary by project and will depend on what I'm prioritizing at the time.

When I was little, my grandfather brought home a necklace he'd found at a yard sale. Its gold-plated pendant said "I'm OK" on one side and "You're OK" on the other. If I had to summarize my thoughts about pantsing versus outlining, I'd do it with those four words. I think that if the story is forming, whether on the page or in our minds, and that if we're giving it the time it deserves, then we are all A-OK. As with the messages on the pendant, there will be times when only one writing approach is visible and working for us, but that doesn't mean that both can't co-exist within the same writer and flip-flop, like my pendant did, throughout a project or a career.

Excerpt

Dead Lift

by

Rachel Brady

Claire Gaston's amber hair rode flat against her head, giving the impression she'd just climbed out of bed. Any make-up had worn away too, yet she still looked closer to forty than her real age—which I knew from her file was fifty-three. In any case, Claire was twenty years my senior, had spent a day and a night in the clink, and still looked better than I did after a comfortable night of sleep and a shower.

We picked up telephone handsets on either side of an opaque window in the jail's visitation room, and I tried to ascertain whether she regarded me with hope or just curiosity.

"I'm Emily Locke," I said, "part of your defense team." I smiled, trying to convey that I withheld judgment, even though I wasn't sure that was true. "Sorry about the circumstances."

She leaned forward and rested her elbows on a countertop that extended away from the dividing window. Richard Cole, the private investigator I worked for, often said that it was a good practice to mirror a subject's body language during interviews, so I did. My forearms ended up in something sticky.

"Are you the investigator my lawyer hired?"

"I'm that investigator's lackey."

She tipped her chin up but didn't speak.

"Hope you don't mind." I pulled a folded paper from my purse. "I brought a list of things to clarify. My boss is painfully deficient with specifics."

"What every woman looks for in an investigator."

"Actually, he's very good. We just work differently."

Claire surveyed the tiny countertop on her side of the glass and brushed invisible debris onto the floor. "Ask away."

"Let's start with your kids."

She inhaled and seemed to hold the breath. "They're all I think about."

"Who's keeping them?"

"My parents." Her gaze fell. "Even though they're too old to be caring for kids." She traced imaginary shapes on the countertop with neatly manicured fingers that reminded me of my best friend Jeannie's hands. "You probably know I'm in the middle of a divorce."

She glanced up long enough to see me nod.

"Daniel's not their father. My second husband, Ruben, moved back to Argentina last year. Our custody fight was...I'm ashamed of it. And now with me here—" she looked around our tiny, divided cubicle— "he'll come back and take them away, I know it. I didn't kill Wendell Platt. You have to help me prove it before Ruben swoops in and disappears with the boys."

"It would help me to understand what's going on with Daniel."

Claire leaned back and crossed her arms. Richard would have said I'd put her on the defensive.

"What does he have to do with this?"

I cupped my chin in my hands and watched her for a moment, trying to figure out if she was angry. "Police are reconstructing your day on

Thursday, trying to figure out where you went and what you did before Dr. Platt's murder. I hear you and Daniel had quite a fight."

She straightened and opened her mouth to argue, but I raised a hand and continued.

"We've all said things we didn't mean, don't worry. The trouble's that the police want to interview Daniel but can't find him. You were the last person to see him and witnesses say you were enraged. It doesn't help to have extra suspicion directed at you."

About Rachel Brady

Rachel Brady lives in Houston, Texas, where she works as a research engineer at NASA. Her interests include health and fitness, acoustic guitar, and books of all kinds. *Final Approach* and *Dead Lift* are the first installments in her Emily Locke mystery series, which bases each story in a different sports community. Rachel offers complimentary signed copies of either book to readers or librarians who choose Emily Locke titles for their book clubs. Visit her on-line at www.rachelbrady.net.

Rebecca Cantrell

"Chillingly realistic...There's so much to love...the setting, the characters, the sexual tension...the political and personal betrayals."

—*USA Today*

The world Rebecca Cantrell has chosen for her remarkable Hannah Vogel novels, beginning with A Trace of Smoke, *is Germany during the long, terrifying dusk of the rise and ultimate ascendency of Adolf Hitler. This is a brave choice, I think; a writer who wants to explore this period needs faith in her powers. She needs to be absolutely certain that she won't inadvertently trivialize the tragedy. Rebecca Cantrell rises to the occasion, and that's saying quite a lot.*

The Jewish Journal, *in its review of the second book in the series, said that Cantrell "flawlessly captures Germany's descent into darkness under growing Nazi power." That seems to me to be praise of the highest order, and we haven't even looked at the quality of the stories themselves—but they've gotten stars from all the important star-awarding publications and won both the Macavity and the Bruce Alexander Awards, plus nominations for many others, so I'm not the only one who believes the tales and characters ring true, too—and here's how she creates them.*

Hist.fiction - knows events + setting
Writes first page blind

Don't Spill the Beans

Pantser or plotter?

Don't tell my editor, but I write the first 50 pages blind. I have no idea who the characters are or what they will do. This is in spite of the fact that I had to turn in a synopsis of the book to sell it. I figure nobody read the synopsis and, if they did, they won't remember the details a year later or bust me for it. So far, this has worked. Don't spill the beans.

Because I write historical fiction, I do know when the action takes place and where the characters will be. In fact, I will have researched the era and place for hours and hours and hours and...you get the picture. I have a notebook full of trivia I gleaned from reference books, diaries, newspapers of the era, movies, and pictures I found on the Internet (not that kind of pictures). From that I extract some ideas of cool or truly awful historical events, characters, and facts I might want to put in a book. But that's all.

I sit down with all that background and write 50 pages. I fuel it with soy chais and a soundtrack whose sole purpose is to shut out the noises of everyone in the coffee shop or house around me. I try not to think about what I'm writing or even re-read it at this point. It might never make the final cut, and I don't want to get too attached to it.

I also have a writing journal that I start at about this time. Into it I put:

All my whining: why did I pick 1930s Berlin? What kind of underpants did they even wear? My insecurity: What made me think I could be a writer? I have no idea where I'm going with this and it's all going to collapse in a big stinking pile and I'll have to give back the advance or even worse it'll get published and I'll be thrashed by reviewers and Amazon readers and some old lady will make her dog pee on my shoe, it's so bad.

Plot ideas: what if I have that zeppelin get zeppelin-jacked? Do you think that means I'll be able to convince some zeppelin company to give me a free zeppelin ride? How explosive were those things? If you shot a gun inside, what would happen?

To-do lists: must fold the laundry so that we can find the living room again. Mail off those books. Buy vegetables, and not broccoli again.

After I finish those 50 pages I read them to see if they might actually be part of a novel. If not, I throw them out and write another 50 pages. If so, I start to outline. I outline the whole book, beginning to end. I use index cards that I stick to a board and they fall down and I lose them and also step on the pushpins if I get really lucky.

Then I write another 50 pages. At the end of those I discover that my outline is wrong. The outline is wrong both going forward (i.e., things I haven't written yet) and going backward (i.e., things I have written that weren't in the original outline). More outlining. I write another 50 pages and…you get the idea.

Looking at it put down here, it seems totally crazy, but it is my process. After having sat through many classes on "the writing process" I've discovered only one truth: Your process is your own. Figure out what your process is and honor it.

If you think outlining sucks all the fun out of writing, don't make yourself do it. And remember, they don't really read that synopsis, so don't work yourself up into a frothing frenzy writing it either. If the thought of embarking on a year-long journey of novel writing without any damn idea of what you're doing gives you hives, by all means write an outline. Neither approach is wrong, despite what you may hear.

When I'm all done I match up the outline to the book I wrote so I can keep track of what actually happened. By this point it's all in a calendar. Despite being in a calendar, my timeline invariably gets screwed up and a meticulous member of my writing group always gleefully catches it (thanks, Karen!). Writing groups are a big part of my process. Without my group of trusted readers, who knows if anyone could understand what comes out of my head.

After I get to the end of the book I start rewriting. I rewrite tons as I'm one of those weird writers who writes too little and always has to add new scenes (as opposed to the writers who write too much and have to delete scenes).

Once I have all the scenes I need in the correct order, then I go in and polish my language, my dialogue, my characterization, and my shoes (just checking to see if you finished the sentence). This is painstaking work and not for the faint of heart, but it is absolutely necessary as I don't put down one golden word after another. Maybe someday.

There it is: the good, the bad, and the ugly. My process. And remember, don't tell my editor.

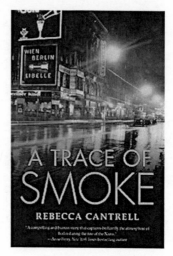

Excerpt

A Trace of Smoke

by

Rebecca Cantrell

Echoes of my footfalls faded into the damp air of the Hall of the Unnamed Dead as I paused to stare at the framed photograph of a man. He was laid out against a riverbank, dark slime wrapped around his sculpted arms and legs. Even through the paleness and rigidity of death, his face was beautiful. A small, dark mole graced the left side of his cleft chin. His dark eyebrows arched across his forehead like bird wings, and his long hair, dark now with water, streamed out behind him.

Watery morning light from high windows illuminated the neat grid of black-and-white photographs lining the walls of the Alexanderplatz police station. One hundred frames displayed the faces and postures of Berlin's most recent unclaimed dead. Every Monday the police changed out the oldest photographs to make room for the latest editions of those who carried no identification, as was too often the case in Berlin since the Great War.

My eyes darted to the words under the photograph that had called to me. Fished from the water by a sightseeing boat the morning of Saturday, May 30, 1931—the day before yesterday. Apparent cause of death: stab wound to the heart. Under distinguishing characteristics they listed a heart-shaped tattoo on his lower back that said "Father." No identification present.

I needed none. I knew the face as well as my own, or my sister Ursula's, with our square jaws and cleft chins. I wore my dark blond hair cut short into a bob, but he wore his long, like our mother, like any woman of a certain age, although he was neither a woman nor of a certain age. He was my baby brother, Ernst.

About Rebecca Cantrell

Rebecca Cantrell writes the award-winning Hannah Vogel mystery series set in 1930s Berlin, including *A Trace of Smoke, A Night of Long Knives, A Game of Lies,* and the forthcoming *A City of Broken Glass.* Her short stories are included in the *First Thrills* anthology. Rebecca also wrote the critically-acclaimed YA iMonsters series, including *iDrakula,* as Bekka Black. Currently, she is hard at work on the first novel in the "Blood Gospel" series with James Rollins. She lives in Hawaii with her husband, her son, and too many geckos to count, and online at www.rebeccacantrell.com and www.bekkablack.com.

Jeffrey Cohen

"Wise, wicked, and witty."

—Larry Gelbart, Emmy-winning and Oscar-nominated creator of M*A*S*H

Jeffrey Cohen makes me laugh out loud, no matter what name he's writing under. This is someone who begins his lengthy Amazon Author Page, which most of us take deadly seriously, "Jeffrey Cohen started life as poor street urchin, orphaned and taken in by a gang of pickpockets led by an older man named Fagin. No, wait. That's someone else, entirely." Obviously, he has to be watched. I've tried my hand at writing (supposedly) funny mysteries and I know how hard it is, but Jeff makes it look easy.

No matter which series it is—the Aaron Tucker mysteries, the classic-movie themed Double Feature mysteries, or the Haunted Guesthouse books (which he writes as E.J. Copperman), Jeff manages both the laughs and the plots—which are doozies—with a distinctive flair. And he's the exception to the rule that former screenwriters always outline.

The Painted Corner

I love to paint myself into a corner.

I don't like to call myself a "pantser," mostly because it brings up unpleasant memories of junior high school, but given the choice between identifying myself that way and saying that I carefully and meticulously outline every move I'm going to make in a new book, I have to go with the colloquial. I "pants."

See, every writer has a style of working. I'm not talking about the words we choose or the artistry of our construction. I mean the thing that gets us going in the morning (or in my case, the late afternoon) and forces us to continue through the spots when we really haven't a clue what the next word is supposed to be. It's not so much the muse—I think you can write whenever you need to, and don't believe in "Writer's Block"—as it is the motivator, something that keeps you going when there's a ballgame on TV and a bag of Cheetos in the kitchen cabinet.

For me, it wouldn't work if I knew everything that was going to happen in my story before I wrote it. I'd feel like that story had been told. There would be no surprises for me in the process, and no surprises would mean no enjoyment. I might just as well be punching a time clock and working for Da Man instead of this cushy life of skimpy advances and the constant threat of unemployment.

I came from screenwriter's training; I started by writing a truckload of screenplays and trying for years to sell them, with varying degrees of no success. But what I was unable to obtain in monetary compensation I more than made up for with the storytelling technique and confidence I found in endless rewrites and repetition (sadly, however, my utility supplier was not interested in being paid with storytelling technique and confidence). I found out about the three-act structure, what a midpoint was and why it was important, the absolute need for character, and how to write dialogue that didn't sound like people making speeches and more important, didn't always sound like me talking. I'm grateful for everything I learned writing screenplays. Someday, I might try it again, just to see how not selling one feels at this age.

What I found out is that there's no right way to write. There's no wrong way, either. There's only your way. I found mine by doing it—I started with a story idea, a premise, and worked from there once I got the process going. I generally wrote in the late afternoon because when I tried to do it earlier in the day, I'd procrastinate until the late afternoon, and then get all my work in from four to six. So now I work on my "day job," newspaper articles, teaching and like that, until four, and then get to writing the novel. Because there's no sense in wasting all that time when I could be trying to make tuition money for my kids.

Now, I know what I need to start a story—a premise, a character I understand, and a few scenes that I know I want to write. I have an idea where they'll fit in the structure of the story, but not what will connect them to each other. So when I'm writing, if a character does or says something unexpected, I can run with it, rather than trying to cut out something that could be interesting just because it doesn't fit the preset outline I would have concocted before starting in to work.

For example: My second novel, the Aaron Tucker mystery *A Farewell to Legs*, involved our intrepid hero, a freelance reporter and family man trying his best not to investigate crimes, investigating a crime that took place in Washington, DC. Specifically, the murder of a sleazy lobbyist found in his mistress' bed with a kitchen knife sticking out of his chest. And Aaron, who lived in New Jersey, had to go to Our Nation's Capital to investigate. He started by contacting the local police detective working the case, and got remarkably little information, mostly because the cop didn't want to tell him anything.

But Aaron had a somewhat acerbic nature (imagine!) and liked to irritate people to get what he needed. He needled the cop about a high-profile case—like this being too much for the police to handle, and how he was sure they were behind the times in crime investigation. At one point, Aaron suggested the police had not even collected any DNA samples to help identify the killer. And sure enough, the cop was rankled enough to respond.

Now, keep in mind: I really am just looking for a plot point to end the chapter here. Something that will keep the pages turning. And I have not planned ahead, so I don't really know where this is going, but I figure if I keep it going long enough, it'll get somewhere.

The cop told Aaron that they had, too, gotten DNA samples, and one of them had paid off: A hair belonging to a man convicted of a series of murders in Texas some years before.

Terrific, Aaron said, you've got your man. So go arrest him.

We can't, the cop answered. The guy was executed by the Texas State Troopers seven years ago.

And I got finished typing that, read it, and honest to goodness, said aloud, "What?"

But here's the thing: I decided I liked that bit. So now I had to figure out how it made sense in the context of my story. And while I'm not going to tell you how I resolved it (go ahead and buy the damn thing; I've got kids to send to college and it's now available as an audiobook!), I will tell you that I'm pretty proud of how it came out.

It wouldn't have happened if I'd outlined meticulously ahead of time and slavishly stuck to the outline. I'm not suggesting that all those who write outlines do that; some are quite flexible, and can change the outline when necessary. They are using one just because they like to have a road map, and I respect that.

But for me, the thrill of the hunt isn't as much fun if the fox and the dogs have worked out the capture among themselves ahead of time. I thrive on the discovery process. As I write, I find out things about my characters that can have an impact on the plot. That helps me keep the characters front and center, and have the plot serve them, rather than the other way around.

That's just my process. Yours is yours. You should do what works for you.

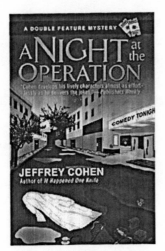

Excerpt

A Night at the Operation

by

Jeffrey Cohen

"Sharon is missing."

I looked up from what I'd been doing—playing an addictive little computer game called MacBrickout—and that resulted in a double punishment for me. First, I lost the ball that was knocking out a series of increasingly hard-to-hit bricks on my computer screen. Second, I was now looking at the face of Dr. Gregory Sandoval, my ex-wife's soon-to-be-second-ex-husband, who was standing in the doorway of my office, uninvited.

"What do you mean, 'missing?'" I asked. I actually do know what "missing" means, but I was caught off-guard and hadn't really been listening to Gregory. I try to not listen to Gregory whenever possible.

The thing about Gregory is: I have tried, on numerous occasions, to pretend he doesn't exist, but there is scientific evidence that he does. The man is an irritant, like a tiny speck of dust in your eye that won't wash out no matter how much Visine you use.

Of course, he was wrong. Sharon was not missing. I'd seen my ex-wife only the day before.

It hadn't been a pleasant experience, but I couldn't blame that on Sharon, nor, even more surprisingly, myself. The fact is that after the age of twenty-two or so, and maybe even before, it's just no fun to get a physical examination.

I go to my ex-wife's medical practice for a number of reasons. First, I know that Sharon and Antoinette Westphal, who started the practice, invite only the best doctors they know to join them. Second, it is convenient to where I work and where I live. Third, I get to see Sharon, with whom I have a cordial divorce, whenever I go there.

And last but not least, I still get the family discount. A man paying for his own health insurance worries about such things.

But that doesn't carry much comfort with it when you're a man in his late thirties and another man is checking you for signs of testicular cancer. It's hard to think of much else at a time like that.

About Jeffrey Cohen

Jeff Cohen has written nine published mystery novels under his own name. In the Aaron Tucker series are *For Whom the Minivan Rolls*, *A Farewell to Legs* and *As Dog Is My Witness*. In the Double Feature series are *Some Like It Hot-Buttered*, *It Happened One Knife*, and *A Night At the Operation* with one more coming in February 2013. Several others are in various stages of development. His books have been translated into English by very kindly editors who read his first drafts. Under the name E.J. Copperman (don't get him started on the name thing), he now writes the Haunted Guesthouse mystery series (*Night of the Living Deed* and *An Uninvited Ghost*), most recently represented by *Old Haunts*. *Chance of a Ghost*, the fourth in the series, will be published early in 2013. He's also written, under his own name, for many newspapers and magazines. His hobbies include speaking about himself in the third person.

Meredith Cole

"This debut novel is likely to be the start of a bright career, as it is clever, original and eminently readable.... This is a story that lingers after the final chapter."

—*San Jose Mercury Press*

All published writers go through the thrill of being put into print for the first time, but very few of them have that debut book published by winning a competition among hundreds, if not thousands, of manuscripts—and then see that same book go on to be a finalist for one of the mystery genre's most important honors.

But all of that happened to Meredith Cole, who won the Minotaur and Malice Domestic competition for Best Traditional Mystery with Posed for Murder, *which was promptly nominated for the Agatha Award, probably the most prestigious honor for traditional whodunnits.*

A "traditional" mystery is one that's written in the spirit of the Golden Age: it's not hard-boiled, it's not gratuitously sexy—and it plays fair with the reader, who is presumably competing with the author, trying to solve the crime before the detective reveals all. These are much trickier books to write than thrillers, so it's reassuring to me as a writer to know that someone as good at classical mysteries as Cole is, wouldn't think of working without an outline.

Outliner

To Outline or Not to Outline

When I teach mystery writing to fledgling writers at the University of Virginia, I encourage all of my students to make an outline. I think it's easy for a first-timer to get so enthusiastic that they plunge immediately into their story, and then at the first sign of trouble they stop. And don't start again. An outline is a great way for them to find their way through the dark. They know where they're headed, so they can start figuring out how to get from here to there.

I am, without a doubt, an outliner. It very likely originates from my tendency to make lists. I like to know where I'm going and what I need to do to get there in my day-to-day life and in my fiction. That certainly doesn't mean I can't deviate a bit on my way. I'm open to bursts of creativity, brand new ideas and exciting twists and turns. But first I like to start with a rough road map.

When I say outline, please don't imagine some sort of list with Roman numerals. I think I had to do outlines like that in 6th grade. My outlines are really a collection of thoughts that grow from a central idea. I continue to expand on my outline in a Word document. I add to it as new plot points occur to me, and write little snippets of description and dialogue when they come to me. Eventually this collection of thoughts begins to get long enough to start to divide it into chapters. I start to see where I need to expand my story and what pieces of the plot I need to connect. I look over the whole picture, and fix story problems before I become attached to the carefully crafted words on the page.

Even as I start to write my book, I keep my outline at the end of the manuscript so I can consult it as needed. This helps when I have to stop writing and then start again (interrupted by my family, galleys for my previous book, or any number of things). I continue to add to the end of it as I go, writing short notes for myself to look at later about inconsistencies or ideas to add in on the second draft.

I know lots of writers who say they don't outline, and some of them probably actually do write by the seat of their pants (and consequently admit to doing a lot of revising). I admire their ability to keep a whole novel in their head. I just can't do it. And I've heard a few writers say that outlining makes writing the book itself boring. But I keep getting surprised by my story, even when I'm revising, so I don't get that at all.

Interestingly enough, quite a few non-outliners I've spoken to admit to doing something similar to my process. They just don't call it outlining for some reason. Perhaps they think that outlining involves those dreaded Roman numerals, and is less organic and creative.

I recently started a new book that borrows the basic plot line from one of my abandoned novels. I began to write the book without outlining. I knew the story well, so at first it seemed as if it would be no problem. But I wrote myself quickly into a couple of dead ends, got my timeline all messed up and had to start tweaking at the midway point. So now I'm back to my original method. It keeps me writing until it's time to type "the end," and that's what's most important.

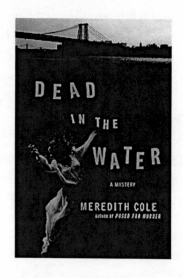

Excerpt

Dead in the Water

by

Meredith Cole

The park was quiet for a Sunday afternoon. The weather had been hot, steamy and still all week, and she imagined everyone who could was staying in enjoying their air conditioning. A Hasidic family, three kids in matching navy blue outfits and a baby in the pram, sat on a park bench. A lone trumpeter played a bluesy number apparently for the sheer joy of hearing it echo off the walls of the nearby Domino Sugar factory. A tan pit bull sniffed around the trash cans while his hipster owner chatted on a cell phone. Despite the available trashcans, the visitors to the park had managed to drop a lot of garbage all over that weekend. Lydia was still amazed at how lazy people could be, dropping trash sometimes right in front of a garbage can.

Lydia set out for the rocks lining the water. There was always a slight breeze off the river, and it lifted up her shoulder length bright red hair and cooled off her neck. She was annoyed to see more garbage floating in the water.

She climbed closer, wondering if it was something she could remove with a stick. A wave from a passing motorboat lifted it up and a pale hand floated to the surface.

Lydia froze. She wondered briefly if she was seeing things. What had looked like a large piece of trash was actually a body. She scrambled closer hoping briefly that it was someone who could be saved and revived, someone who might have just fallen in. But the hand floated again, lifeless to the surface.

About Meredith Cole

Meredith Cole started her career as a screenwriter and filmmaker. She was a New York Foundation for the Arts fellow in Screenwriting and directed several feature films. Cole won the St. Martin's Press/Malice Domestic competition, and her book, *Posed for Murder*, was published by St. Martin's Minotaur in 2009. She was nominated for an Agatha Award for Best First Mystery Novel in 2010. Her second book, *Dead in the Water*, continues the adventures of photographer and amateur sleuth Lydia McKenzie in Brooklyn. Cole's short stories have been published in Ellery Queen Mystery Magazine and in anthologies. Her website is www.culturecurrent.com/cole.

Bill Crider

"Few will be able to resist Crider's brand of broad humor, eccentric characters, and murder."

—*Publishers Weekly*

Bill Crider is an inspiration to novelists everywhere. Living quietly in Alvin, Texas, not calling much attention to himself, he turns out wonderful book after wonderful book – more than fifty of them so far—and a whole lot of people, myself included, are waiting for more. Crider has written horror, westerns, and, of course, mysteries, including the Sheriff Dan Rhodes series, the Carl Burns series, the Truman Smith series, the Sally Good series, and the Stanley Waters series, co-written with television personality Willard Scott. And along the way, he's piled up a bunch of Awards nominations, including the Edgar and the Shamus, and he's won two Anthonys and a Derringer.

Crider's books remind me (this may startle him) of the work of one of my favorite of all writers, Anthony Trollope. Both writers create an ultimately sound and moral world (although a world in which things can go wildly wrong) and both have a way of assuring the reader that the person behind the book is real, solid, and dependable. And writes really good stories.

Begin At the Beginning and Go On Until You Come to the End

When it comes to writing, I'm a seat-of-the-pants kind of a guy. Here's why. When I started writing, I didn't know any better. I thought writing was like telling a story, and I thought that when you told a story, you just started telling it and found out what happened as you went along. That's the way I told stories when I was a kid. It was the way my aunt told stories to me and my brother and my sister when she visited at our grandmother's house in the summers. I had no idea that anybody would actually sit down and plan a story before it was told.

Even after I started writing and selling, I didn't know any better. The world was different in those days. No Internet, no e-mail, no writing conferences. Those things were in their infancy, and before too long they'd be accessible to everyone, but I was just a guy living in Alvin, Texas, teaching college during the daytime and writing books at night. What did I know? Nothing much, except that when I was a college student myself, there was a reading room in The University of Texas library with lovely decorated rafters. Besides being decorated, the rafters had quotations on them, and one of them was this, from *Alice in Wonderland*: "Begin at the beginning and go on till you come to the end: then stop." It seemed like great advice to me, and I thought it applied to storytelling, no matter what its context in Lewis Carroll's book.

That's not to say I've never used an outline. I have. When writing under house names for a certain fiction factory, I was supposed to provide a lengthy outline for the books I turned in. I believe that thirty pages was the required amount. As I recall, I always came up a little short, and that was in spite of my taking up at least three pages with a cast of characters.

Around that same time, I wrote a few novels in the M.I.A. Hunter series. Steve Mertz, the originator of the series, always provided an outline for me. The outlines were only a couple of pages long, though, which seemed perfect to me. They allowed me plenty of room to tell things my own way.

For that matter, so did the thirty-page outlines. After they were approved, I hardly ever looked at them again. I just started at the beginning and kept on going.

It doesn't take much to get me started. When I wrote *Dead on the Island*, the first novel in my series about a private-eye named Truman Smith, all I had was the opening line: "There was no one on the seawall except for me and the rat." I'd been inspired by my young niece who'd spent some time in Galveston, staying at the oldest and grandest hotel on the island, swimming in the Gulf of Mexico, and playing on the beach. When I saw her, she didn't want to talk about any of that. The thing that had impressed her was the rat she'd seen on the seawall. I told my wife that someday I'd use that rat in a book, and a couple of years later I sat down and wrote that first line.

And that was all I had. That line, and the idea that I was going to write a first-person private-eye novel. I typed the line, and then I kept on going until I came to the end.

The same thing happened with another book, *Murder Most Fowl*. One day I jogged past a nursing home and a little old guy yelled at me from the porch: "Somebody stole my teef!" A good many years later, I sat down to write a Sheriff Dan Rhodes book. I typed that line, and, well, you know the rest.

Is it scary to begin with only a single line and nothing more? You're durned tootin', but sometimes that's the way it works for me. Sometimes I have a little more. I have a situation that I want to write about or I have a crime that I think would make an interesting starting point. Sometimes I even think I know how the book will develop and what the ending will be. Usually when I think that, I'm wrong.

There are times when I really wish I were an outliner, a meticulous planner who's always in control of a book's direction. But I'm not. I seldom even know what characters will turn up from page to page. They just appear and start acting or talking, and I try to keep up with them. Usually by the time I'm about halfway through the book, I do know pretty well what's going on and what's going to happen, but even that's not a sure thing.

So if I just start with a line or a vague idea, where do the books come from? Am I drawing from some deep well of the unconscious? And if I am, should I start paying my unconscious 10% of the take? I honestly have no idea how to answer those questions. Sometimes I think that if I could answer them, I'd have to stop writing. That might prove to be easier than I think. If I never wrote that first line, I'd likely never think of the rest of it.

By the way, in case you were wondering, I wrote this little essay the same way I do everything else. As an old English teacher, I should probably be ashamed.

Excerpt

The Wild Hog Murders

by

Bill Crider

(Sheriff Dan Rhodes has just told Hack Jensen, the dispatcher, and Lawton, the jailer, about the events leading up to his discovery of a murder victim, a man Rhodes had been pursuing because he stole some gas at a local convenience store.)

"So the car's in the impound lot already, and there's one man dead and another one on the run," Hack said. "That about it?"

"That's about it," Rhodes agreed.

"All because some fella stole some gas," Lawton said. "That's just not right."

"There was more to it than the gas," Rhodes said. "There's always more to it when somebody gets shot."

"The fella that got away," Hack said.

"What about him?"

"You think he did it?"

"He's the number one suspect," Rhodes said.

"What about those hunters?" Lawton said. "I saw this movie once about some fellas that stumbled onto a bunch of hunters. Didn't turn out so good for 'em."

"'Deliverance?'" Hack said.

"Coulda been. I think a hog was mentioned in that."

"Was a pig. Burt Reynolds sure was good in that one."

"That other guy didn't come out so well," Lawton said. "What was his name?"

"Ned Beatty," Rhodes said.

"That's the one," Lawton said. "Felt sorry for him."

"Good thing you didn't stay out there in those woods all by yourself tonight," Hack said. "What with them hunters roamin' around and all."

Rhodes thought about the gunshots he'd heard just before the hog stampede. He hadn't thought about the shots again because of all the excitement that had come right afterward, but now he did. There'd been too many shots for the hunters to be shooting at the hogs. Something else had been going on. He'd have to remember that tomorrow.

"Nothin' like that movie could happen here," Lawton said.

"I wouldn't count on it," Hack said.

About Bill Crider

Bill Crider lives in scenic Alvin, Texas, near Houston and the Texas Gulf Coast, where he's suffered the effects of both Hurricane Ike and

Hurricane Alicia. He was the Division Chair of English and Humanities at Alvin Community College before his retirement in 2002.

Bill is the author of more than fifty published novels and numerous short stories. He won the Anthony Award for best first mystery novel in 1987 for *Too Late to Die*. He and his wife, Judy, won the best short story Anthony in 2002 for their story "Chocolate Moose." His story "Cranked" from *Damn Near Dead* (Busted Flush Press) was nominated for the Edgar award, the Anthony Award, and the Derringer Award. It won the latter. He's won the Golden Duck Award for best juvenile science fiction novel and been nominated for a Shamus. His latest novel is *The Wild Hog Murders* (St. Martin's). Interested readers might check out *The Blacklin County Files, Dead on the Island, The Prairie Chicken Kill* and *When Old Men Die*. Check out his homepage at http://www.billcrider.com or take a look at his peculiar blog at http://billcrider.blogspot.com.

Jeremy Duns

"The immediacy of Duns' writing grabs and suspends the reader in a beautifully realized heartbeat of recent history."

—*Kirkus Reviews*

There's a great tradition in the art of the espionage novel, and Jeremy Duns is dead center in it, while staking ownership of new territory, all his own.

The major themes of spy fiction, it seems to me, are loyalty, betrayal, deception, self- deception, and identity. Identity is, of course, central: who is the spy? Is he the person others —on both sides of the ideological divide—believe him to be? Is he the person he believes himself to be? Paul Dark, the hero of Duns' trilogy about a Cold War spy, is adrift in many ways, cut off even from a full understanding of his own beginnings. Those around him may have no more depth or reality than shadow puppets. For spies like Dark, caught between the massive grinding stones of the great powers, the primary imperative is survival.

Duns is a master of the plot reversal, but it's character and atmosphere that resonate most profoundly in his work. We are in a renaissance of the espionage novel, and Jeremy Duns is very much a part of it.

(And his listing of qualities he wants his novel to embody is, I think, a really original idea.)

Writes by the seat of pants

never outlined
— now does

Get There

I've written three novels and am now researching my fourth, and each time it's been different, but generally speaking, I'm a "pantser," i.e., I write by the seat of my pants. I usually write a synopsis that takes me through each chapter, but I don't go into too much detail and it changes a lot as I go along. Writing the novel is my outline. I wrote my first book in a more linear way, and got into problems as a result. Now I start by writing tons of notes, ideas, fragments of scenes, snatches of dialogue, and when I've built up a large body of words, 40,000 or so, the structure starts to solidify.

At this point I tend to lose a lot of material as I realize that some scenes weren't as exciting plot developments as I thought they would be, or simply don't fit with other developments that I prefer. That can be frustrating, but I console myself with the thought that if I had prepared a very detailed plot outline in advance I'd have made the same or similar mistakes, but with heavier consequences: I usually cut material that is still only partially formed, so it's less of a sacrifice. One of the reasons I don't write very detailed outlines is because I'm worried I'll change my mind later. Something might seem perfect right now but in three months I might wake up in the middle of the night with the realization that it's completely wrong. Or perhaps not even wrong: perhaps I'll just be bored of the idea by then.

I want to write the kind of books I like to read, and they involve suspense. I've written a trilogy in the first person, and my character is a secret agent in trouble: so to a certain extent I also have to be in trouble. I like twists, but I find they're often most effective if, like my narrator, I don't see them coming. I want to know my protagonist, inside and out, but then to throw him into impossible situations and see how he gets out of them. I find plotting out too much in advance can suck the spontaneity and intensity from my writing, and I value both of those features above most others.

That said, I usually have a few plot points or scenes I want to include going in. With my first novel, *Free Agent*, I knew before I started writing that it would be set in the Biafran War and told from the perspective of a double agent. I also knew roughly how it began and ended, and had an idea of what kind of novel I wanted it to be. I nearly wrote 'clear idea', but it wasn't really clear. It was strong. Just as you can wake with a very vague or even no memory of the dream you just had, but nevertheless have a very powerful sense of the mood of it, I had known in my gut what I wanted to write. I can articulate it now as, roughly, something that had the following elements and tones:

Taut Lean Gripping Spy thriller
Set in the late 60s
Cold War tensions to the fore
In Africa – feel the heat and the culture
Suspenseful action scenes that can match Bourne and Bond
But also character studies that are more like Greene or le Carré
So no silly gadgets or explosions
Dark, gritty and bleak
Conflicted and trapped first-person narrator
Laconic humor laced in
Real Cold War and espionage history integrated and revealed
Real history of this forgotten civil war
Unusual love story/obsession

Along with a few specific plot and character ideas and sense-memories from my childhood in Nigeria, I carried most of the above with me the whole time I wrote *Free Agent* – without ever writing them down as I just have. But when my drafts were nowhere near reaching the above, my instincts pushed me to make it happen. I felt that as long as I kept writing I would be able to fill in all the gaps and make the impression I had of the novel a reality.

With my second and third books, I wrote down a lot more about what kind of novels I wanted them to be before I started writing. But I still wanted to keep something of the feel I was looking for unarticulated, held back in my subconscious. With the second, *Song of Treason*, my thoughts about setting changed early on, which entailed a lot more research. But in each case I've had clear ideas about the beginning and end, some strong impressions of the tone of the books, of the mood of my protagonist and what's at stake for him and those around him.

My methodology changed somewhat between writing my first and second novels: it became less structured. I wrote *Free Agent* in the evenings and weekends, handing in new chapters to a writing group as I went along. I wrote *Song of Treason* as a full-time author in a year. I was naturally worried that it wouldn't be as good as my first, which took me around seven years to write (albeit with a full-time job and no external deadline). So I attacked the second in a very different way: I thought a lot and researched a lot, then worked out a very rough synopsis and started writing, 1,000 words a day, throwing anything and everything down. It helped that I felt I had succeeded in my goals with *Free Agent*. Not only had it been accepted by a publisher, who had then shown faith in me by buying the next two books in the trilogy, but I felt that I had written the book I had wanted to. So I had a lot more faith in myself that I would get where I wanted, eventually. This helped when I became blocked or encountered problems.

Not having a very detailed outline means you will encounter problems, but I don't think you can necessarily work your way out of them with outlines. At least, I don't think I can. I think in drafting a novel it may be that there comes a point where structure, character and plot are almost irrelevant, or rather that they are no longer concrete or tangible to the writer. You can prepare very carefully and research and plot everything out, but at some point your instinct comes into play. For want of a better word, you feel the book. You realize what it needs, what it's missing, and you set to work giving it that. You're not really thinking about why a certain idea or scene or even line will make sense. You just feel that it will. Sometimes I can be blocked for weeks, and wish I had been more organized at the outset and had done a 'proper' outline of the book, scene by scene. But then I can make enormous strides in minutes, changing the book with very radical decisions that months earlier I would have been terrified of making, but which now, somehow, I know will work. This isn't something you can put on index cards. It's about living the book, with all its problems and setbacks. Index cards and detailed outlining work fantastically well for some writers, but they're not for me, and there's no shame in it. All writers are working around a group of ideas until they manage to craft a piece they are proud of and prepared to send out into the world – it doesn't really matter how we get there, as long as we do.

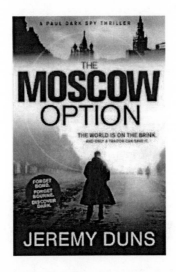

Excerpt

The Moscow Option

by

Jeremy Duns

Late October 1969, Moscow, Soviet Union

I was asleep when they came for me. I was running through a field, palm trees in the distance, when I woke to find a man shaking my shoulders and yelling my name.

I sat bolt upright, gasping for breath, sweat pouring off me. The man was wearing a cap, and looked to be barely out of his teens. Part of my mind was still caught up in the dream: I was sure I'd been in the field before, but couldn't think when or where. But I didn't get the chance to consider it further because I was being hauled from the mattress by my arms. Now I could see that there were two men, both in the same uniform but one without a cap. Neither was part of my usual guard detail.

'Get up, scum!' shouted the one in the cap, leaning in so close that he was just a couple of inches from me. His face was squared off, with a wide jawline and a pug nose, and he was wearing some foul eau de cologne that seemed to have been impregnated with the scent of fir trees rolled in diesel. He shoved a pile of clothes into my arms.

'Put these on, old man,' he sneered. 'And make it fast.'

About Jeremy Duns

Jeremy Duns is the author of the Paul Dark spy thrillers. His first novel, *Free Agent*, received a starred review from *Publishers Weekly*, was a *Daily Telegraph* Thriller of the Year 2009, and received praise from William Boyd, Eric Van Lustbader and David Morrell while *The Guardian* wrote: "Deep knowledge of espionage and classic spy novels informs this excellent debut." *The Times* called the second book in the series, *Song of Treason*, "a masterly excursion back to the bad old days of the Cold War," while *The Guardian* said it was "a treat for fans of traditional Len Deighton-style spy thrillers." *The Dark Chronicles*, an omnibus of the trilogy, was published in 2012. His next book is *The Spy of The Century*, a non-fiction investigation of the Oleg Penkovsky espionage operation. Jeremy lives in Sweden. Find out more at http://jeremyduns.blogspot.com and http://www.jeremyduns.com.

Leighton Gage

"...top notch... controversial... entirely absorbing... irresistible."

—*The New York Times*

Leighton Gage writes highly atmospheric, almost surreally visual books set against the astonishing extremes of Brazil. When I read him, I often have the sensation that I'm seeing a very tightly lighted and somewhat confined reality, and that beyond the edges of the light is a world of riotous color, as extravagant, fantastic, and dangerous as a coral reef. The painter that comes to mind is Henri Rousseau.

But that world is mostly in shadow; it's what we probably think of as the wilder and more perilous Brazil, although the crimes we watch are often grim enough to cast that into doubt. They're investigated by one of fiction's most decent and most convincing cops, Chief Inspector Mario Silva, who has to struggle not only against the perpetrators but also a poisonous political environment in which expedience is the quickest way to promotion. The Wall Street Journal *called the Silva books, "A world-class procedural series," and it's difficult to disagree.*

Falling All Over It: An Interview

Q: The world is divided (roughly) between pantsers, who make it up as they go along, and plotters, who plot, or even outline, in advance. Where do you fall on that spectrum?

A: I fall all over it. It's a consequence of stumbling. And what I generally stumble over is first drafts. My first novel (deservedly unpublished) was created without forethought to plot and without any kind of an outline. That was back in my who needs a freakin' outline stage.

Uh, maybe I did. The only good thing about that book was the title. (*Amazon Snow*. Catchy, huh?) Well, hell, I thought it was catchy.

The second book ultimately became *Blood of the Wicked*. Why "ultimately?" Because, again, I didn't do any plotting, I didn't outline, and the first draft wound-up being one long outline. As an outline, it was pretty good. As a book, it sucked.

In the famous speech Churchill gave on the occasion of his very first entrance into the House of Commons as Britain's new Prime Minister, he said, "I would say to the House, as I said to those who have joined the government: I have nothing to offer but blood, toil, tears and sweat."

"Blood, toil, tears and sweat," the man said. What an inspiration! I already had the blood. It was in the title, and there were gallons more between the pages. All I had to do, I figured, was to add the toil, tears and sweat. So I toiled. And toiled. And used up lots of handkerchiefs and cans of deodorant spray. Revision followed revision, rewrite followed rewrite. At last it was good enough to publish, was published and, *mirabile dictu*, got a favorable mention in the *New York Times*.

The experience taught me two things, one of them about publicity, the other about writing:

1. Not plotting, or outlining, can snag you a mention in the *New York Times*.

2. Not plotting or outlining, can waste you a hell of a lot of time.

Confusing, huh? Well, crap, it was for me too.

Confession time: I am, by nature, lazy and loath to put any more effort into anything than I absolutely have to.

Fact: I am a perfectionist; averse to turning in any manuscript that isn't as good as I can get it.

Mutually exclusive? Um, not really. But confusing for some, my wife for starters. I am reminded of a cartoon I once saw in The New Yorker:

A sculptor is up on a ladder, hammer and chisel in hand. The huge statue in front of him is split right down the middle. His wife is looking up at him. Her line: "You never learn, do you, Pierre? You and your 'one more tap'."

Can you "improve" a book to death? Some people think so. My wife sure as hell thinks so. I don't.

But maybe, just maybe (thought I to myself upon concluding book #1), there's a way to maintain quality and save myself some work.

Enter the outline. I decided to give it a try. And it works for me.

Q: Why does it work for you?

A: Because I have learned, the hard way, not to show my outlines to anyone. Maybe you, dear fellow writers, have a different experience. But mine has been that people, certain people, certain important-in-the-process people (not just wives) often start putting in their two cents on the outline. Yeah, on the outline; saves them the trouble of having to wait and read the book.

Does me no good to explain that I never follow an outline exactly, that I keep changing the story as I go along. They're going to put in their two cents anyway.

Advice to newbies: outline, but tell people you don't.

Q: How do you actually approach it?

A: Even with six books behind me, I still feel like a newbie, still developing my technique. One thing that seems to be working at the moment, at least it has with my last two books, is to begin with the end and outline backward. Does that make sense to you?

If it doesn't, I'm not gonna bother to explain it. Reading my explanation would be a waste of your time because, if you don't get it straightaway, you're not likely to even after I've thrown a lot of words at it.

Q: Where do you think your stories come from?

A: I'm fortunate to be living in a country where a lot of weird stuff happens. My first book, for example, deals with liberation theology and land reform. You got liberation and land reform at work in your country?

Ha! I didn't think so.

Here's how the story came about: One starry Brazilian night, I was sharing some wine with a friend of mine, a defrocked priest, also a committed liberation theologian. As the evening progressed, and a long evening it was, he told me many stories of his experiences during Brazil's most recent dictatorship. Hey, I thought, those stories would make a great book. About a week after that, I was splitting a few bottles of Argentinean red with a relative of my wife's while he told me how his ranch was invaded by a group of landless workers. Hey, I thought, that story would make another great book. Still another week went by. My wife went out with a few girlfriends and left me alone with a book about Bishop Oscar Romero and a full magnum of Chilean cabernet. I finished the book, made good progress on the wine, and, for some inexplicable reason, found that all the stories were getting mixed up in my head.

That's when the epiphany occurred: Why bother to try to sort the freakin' things out. Everything together is gonna make a great book.

Three weeks, two conversations, one book, a half-dozen bottles of wine. It was as simple as that. But I should have outlined.

My second opus, *Buried Strangers*, had its origins in a conversation I had in the kitchen of our home. I heard this story about organ theft from

Geralda, one of our maids. As I recall, she was washing dishes and I... hey, that's right, I was drinking a caipirinha.

Maybe it isn't outlining that's the writer's best friend. Maybe it's booze.

Excerpt

Blood of the Wicked

by

Leighton Gage

Father Angelo settled back in his chair, rested his elbows on the arms and took another puff. "Where were you on the thirteenth of May, 1976?" he asked.

It seemed like an abrupt departure from the subject, but Silva played along. "I have no idea. Should I have reason to remember?"

"Probably not. But I do. I can remember exactly where I was on the thirteenth of May, 1976. I was with Anton Brouwer. He would have been..."—he took another puff and made the calculation in his head—

"twenty-four at the time. The two of us were suspended by our wrists, facing each other, in the cellar of the State Police headquarters in Cascatas. They hung us up on the evening of the twelfth. They took us down on the morning of the fourteenth. They had us hanging there for thirty-four hours."

"Why?"

The priest went on as if he hadn't heard the question. "I've always kept a diary. My memoirs. I hope to have them published some day. But I never wrote about that. The whole period of our most recent military dictatorship isn't covered in any degree of detail anywhere in my writings. It was too dangerous to write about then, and I can't bring myself to write about it now. But I talk about it, every now and then. I talk about it to someone like you, someone I don't know too well, or to someone I think should hear the story, and remember. Am I boring you?"

"Not at all."

Father Angelo lit another cigarette from the glowing stub of his last and extinguished the stub in the overflowing ashtray. He dangled the cigarette in his mouth while he rubbed the ash off his fingers. Then he took another puff and went on.

About Leighton Gage

Leighton Gage has lived and worked on six continents, speaks five languages and has written books in two. The *Wall Street Journal* called his work "world-class;" the *Toronto Globe and Mail* found it "masterful," *The Boston Globe* referred to it as "compelling" and *The Florida Sun-Sentinel* dubbed it "fascinating, complex and riveting." His novels have garnered starred reviews from all four of the major trade publications (*Publishers Weekly, Booklist, Library Journal* and *Kirkus*) and have been translated into Finnish, Dutch, Spanish, French and Italian. He lives in a small town near São Paulo. Available now on Kindle are *Blood of the Wicked, Buried Strangers, Dying Gasp, Every Bitter Thing, A Vine in the Blood,* and, most recently, *Perfect Hatred.*

Timothy Hallinan

"Timothy Hallinan is a writer's writer."

—*New York Times* Bestselling author John Lescroart

Introduction by Brett Battles

A few weeks ago, a man in his eighties or so walked up to me in the Farmer's Market as I was reading a book while I ate lunch. "That any good?" he asked.

Looking up, I said, "It's great."

"I like the title. Where's the author from?"

"He's American," I told him.

When he frowned I knew something was up. "There are no really good American writers. Story tellers, sure, but that's it."

I won't go into the rest of the conversation, but when he asked me to name one good American writer who was more than just a story teller, I held up the book I was reading.

The book was The Fear Artist, *and the author, Tim Hallinan. In my mind, Tim is both one of the best writers and storytellers working today. His words are magical. His characters, like friends we wish we had. And his plots, a gorgeous weave of storylines and character arcs and subplots and locations that would seem to have taken him years to work out before he actually begins to write.*

Tim doesn't take years.

There are only three people I'll automatically set down whatever else I might be reading when I get one of their books: Stephen King, Haruki Murakami, and Tim Hallinan.

The Only Method I've Got

For me, character is everything.

I know that sounds like a non sequitur as an opening to a piece about plotting, but it explains why I plot—why I have to plot—in the way I do. I have no choice.

When I say character is everything for me, I mean it literally, To me, plot is what characters do. Dialogue is what characters say. Action is how characters react to challenges. Even setting, I think, is scenery from the characters' perspective.

What that means is that I can't outline. I literally can't imagine what my characters will do in a situation until I'm writing the situation. I don't know what decisions they'll make until they make them. I certainly don't know what they'll say until they say it, and sometimes an entire story will take a sharp turn based on something someone says in what was supposed to be a minor scene. At the beginning of the book, I didn't know the character would say that. I didn't even know I'd be writing the scene—and yet it re-channels the plot of my book.

So, as much as I envy outliners the security of knowing where they're going, I can't emulate them. I'm stuck with a pantsing approach that, reliably as sunrise, leaves me convinced four or five times during the writing of each book that this book can't be finished, and whatever made me think I could write a book in the first place? But I don't have an alternative.

So, okay, this is how I work.

I start with a character or two and a situation. The characters have to interest me, and the situation has to be something that I think will hold my attention for six months to a year, or however long it takes.

Let's take my new Poke Rafferty book, *The Fear Artist*, as an example, since I still remember writing it.

I had been sufficiently upset by the War on Terror to assume that it would hold my interest. What came to me was a question: What happens when someone is caught up, through no fault of his own, in the periphery of the War on Terror, with the potential to become what they euphemistically call "collateral damage," usually meaning dead for no reason?

The thought came during a run one day, and it was solid enough that I started reading. Immediately, I was reminded that Thailand has its own horrific little War on Terror, in response to repeated Islamic fundamentalist violence in the southernmost parts of the Kingdom. So there we are, a local War on Terror for Poke to be caught up in.

That day I wrote the opening sentences:

> Two two-gallon cans of paint weigh about five times as much as he'd thought they would. Feeling as burdened as a prospector's donkey, the wire handles of the cans cutting into his palms, he manages to pull open the door of the shop unaided. The door immediately swings shut on his chest, so he pushes it with his knee and edges through it sideways, left side first. One hundred percent of his attention is focused on not letting the door close on the can in his right hand.
>
> Which means that when he steps onto the wet sidewalk with his back to the road, he's too preoccupied to hear the people running.

In the next instant, the story proper begins as a large foreign man slams into him. The two of them fall to the pavement with Polk underneath; there's a sound like the crack of a bat in a stadium, and the man on top jolts suddenly and rolls off. We realize almost immediately that he's been shot, although the police who show up within seconds deny that to Poke.

What I liked about this was that it got things moving, it happened in a commonplace setting (always the best place for a nightmare to begin), it turned Poke into a guy who just wants to paint his apartment, and the denial of the cops suggested new levels of complexity.

So fine, I thought, he's painting the apartment. Why? Because his wife and adopted daughter, Rose and Miaow, are in the Northeast, visiting Rose's mother. This worked instantly for me because it got the two of them out of the way: I wouldn't have to write a Rose-and-Miaow-in-peril story line.

By the time I was halfway through writing the first chapter, I knew all those things: War on Terror, lying police, murder by sniper, Poke involved accidentally (the man said something to him before he died, and many people want to know what it was), Rose and Miaow in the Northeast. That's a lot of stuff, and the next day I went back and inserted a character in that first scene who would turn out to be the book's number-two villain.

From this point on, writing the book was primarily a matter of showing up every day and following the characters. Poke is lonely and unnerved that night, so he goes to get drunk at a bar frequented by aging sexpats, and he learns more there about what's happening in the south. He goes back home, and there are cops waiting for him. He's hauled downtown and interrogated by the guy I put in the first scene, who wants to know about the time Poke spent in Indonesia and Muslim strongholds in the Philippines, when he was writing a book. The interrogation takes place in front of a one-way mirror, and when Poke barges into the observation room, the book's primary villain is sitting there.

All of this and more—quite a lot of stuff—had materialized by the end of Chapter Three. As I wrote, I continued to read, and up popped the Phoenix Program, a large-scale American assassination campaign in Vietnam in which the CIA and the Army partnered and which was adopted by the Pentagon as one of the foundations of the plan for the War on Terror after 9/11. That discovery gave me the last big element in the book.

Show up, write, follow the characters. I keep a second document, called Bucket, open all the time when I'm working. As ideas for future developments or characters come to me, I either use them right then or switch to the bucket document and make a note. I almost never look at the bucket again because the act of writing the idea down pretty much cements it in place.

I do this every day. On the days when nothing comes, I write anyway, one word after another until I've got 1500 or 2000 of them, no matter how little I enjoy it or how bad it seems to me as I write it. The worst scene on the page (as I said in the introduction to this book) is much better than the best scene in the head, because you can't improve an empty page. Besides, I've made a great discovery, which is that I actually have no idea, while I'm writing, whether it's good or bad. This is very liberating. It lets me keep working even when I think I'm writing junk.

Sometimes—two or three times per book—I get totally stuck. I can't see anything at all. When that happens, I quit for a few days, but I don't write anything else. Something always comes, usually when I'm least expecting it.

My kind of writing is terrifying at times, but I've learned not to give up. It's one of those things—like democracy, a prostate exam, or a mammogram—where you just have to trust the process, however little you enjoy it in the short run.

Anyway, it's the only method I've got.

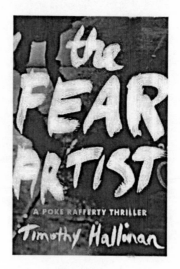

Excerpt

The Fear Artist

by

Timothy Hallinan

Vladimir's eyes lock on something and follow it. He reaches up and smooths his hair. "This is pretty girl," he says, and Rafferty looks up to see Ming Li.

"Get you guys something?" Ming Li says. "You must be Vladimir."

Vladimir says to Rafferty, "She is yours?"

"How old-world," Ming Li says. She looks down at Poke. "Scoot over, whoever you are."

"I'm Poke," Poke says as Ming Li sits. "Vladimir knows my name. Vladimir, this isn't Minnie Lee. Minnie, this isn't really Vladimir."

Vladimir says, "Poke is not a name."

"If you'd told my father that thirty-seven years ago, I'd have been spared a life of shame."

"Poke is better than Philip," Ming Li says. She looks at the envelope in front of Vladimir. "Is that what I think it is?"

Vladimir puts a protective hand on the envelope and says, "That depends on what you think—"

"Money," she says. "You going to earn it?"

Vladimir straightens up an inch or so and looks down his considerable nose at her. "Is already earned."

The two of them examine each other in a way that makes Poke feel he's in the next room. Into the silence, he says, "I wonder how you get a drink in here."

Vladimir says, "You have wery interesting eyes."

Ming Li says, "You've got a nice kind of aging Borat thing going yourself."

"Was a time," Vladimir says mournfully, "you would have chased Vladimir through the woods."

"And caught him, too," Ming Li says.

Poke says, "Would either of you like a—"

"But your eyes," Vladimir says, sliding the envelope back and forth with his fingertips. "Yes, pretty, wery pretty, but interesting."

"I'm just your basic Chinese-American hybrid."

"Glad you guys are getting along," Poke says.

Vladimir says to Poke, "She is baby spy, yes?"

"I'm his bankroll," Ming Li says.

"Yes? And you are knowing him how?"

"I've heard about him my entire life" She laces her fingers together and clasps her hands over her heart. "This is a dream come true."

Vladimir's lower lip comes out half an inch, apparently propelled by doubt. "You are young," he says. "You will have better dream later."

"Hey," Rafferty says. "My life is in danger."

"You guys talk for a minute." Ming Li gets up. "What do you want?"

Rafferty asks for a Singha. Vladimir says, "Wodka. The bottle, please," and watches her cross the room.

"A million dollar, she would be worth to me," Vladimir says. "Two million. Already, I have a hundred ideas."

"Not for sale."

"With fifty like her, look like her, smart like her, I could have won war in Wietnam."

"You did."

"No. Wietnam won. Russia lose ewerything. We lose whole world. We were killed by American telewision." He puckers as though to spit but instead says, "Dallas."

About Timothy Hallinan

Timothy Hallinan is the Edgar and Macavity Award-nominated author of three widely-praised series: the Poke Rafferty Bangkok thrillers, *A Nail Through the Heart*, *The Fourth Watcher*, *Breathing Water*, *The Queen of Patpong*, and *The Fear Artist*; the Junior Bender mysteries, *Crashed*, *Little Elvises*, and *The Fame Thief*; and the six Simeon Grist mysteries, beginning with *The Four Last Things* and *Everything But the Squeal* and concluding with *The Bone Polisher*.

In 2011, Hallinan conceived and edited *Shaken: Stories for Japan*, a collection of short stories by twenty well-known mystery writers, with 100 percent of the proceeds going to tsunami and earthquake relief. He also contributed an extremely well-reviewed short story to the 2011 collection *Bangkok Noir*. He is married to Munyin Choy-Hallinan and lives in Santa Monica and Bangkok.

The largest area of Tim's website is an extensive guide for aspiring writers called "Finish Your Novel."

Gar Anthony Harwood

"...a writer who has always belonged in the upper echelon of American crime fiction."

—Bill Ott, *Booklist*

Gar Anthony Haywood is on the very short list of writers whose new book goes straight to the top of my to-be-read pile, no matter how high and tottering it might be. No matter what he's written, whether it's a gritty noir standalone, a PI series, or a very funny and very compassionate mystery series about an older couple who take to the highways in their Airstream to escape their children, Gar writes his story so beautifully that when I finish it, it seems like that was the only way it could have been written.

Part of that quality is his instinctive (and enviable) economy, and part of it is his voice. We haven't talked much about voice in this book—it might be the topic of a book in itself—but Gar's voice is always natural—whichever of his voices it is. We've all read books in which the writer seems to be straining to be witty or cynical or lyrical or dark; it's easy to see him/her grimacing in effort as the words hit the page. But Gar never seems to exert himself; his voice is measured and effortless, and the sentences flow in what feels like an inevitable sequence.

...'s true, as I think it is, that easy reading means difficult writing, Gar Haywood is one of the hardest-working writers I know. Terrific talent.

...As If I'm Some Kind of Expert

One of the most amazing things about becoming a published author is how instantaneously you transition in the eyes of some from know-nothing wannabe to Professional Literary Figure. One minute you're reading Lawrence Block, wondering if you'll ever live long enough to write a sentence as well as he writes a whole book, and the next you're trading emails with the man and calling him "Larry." That check somebody made out in your name for the honor of publishing your next novel or short story has suddenly made your opinions about the act of writing worth paying attention to, even though they're the same opinions you had the day before, when no one would have given a rat's ass about what you have to say on that or any other subject.

So it is that at times like this, when I've been asked to write something smart and pithy on the "creative process" as if I'm some kind of expert, I agree to do so with a degree of trepidation, because I'm still not sure—even twelve published novels in—that I have any real wisdom to impart. I know what the creative process is like for me; that's about it. If a hundred aspiring authors followed my method of writing to the letter, like the proverbial "infinite number of monkeys" in a room full of typewriters and bond paper, eventually one of them would write a salable manuscript and become a professional author. But that wouldn't be my method proving its worth—that would just be the law of averages doing its thing.

Still. Tim's asked me to write this essay and he's a relatively smart man, so what the hell—here goes.

Where I Get My Ideas

Every published writer I know has at least one snide and thoroughly useless answer to this question at the ready because we hear it so often it's impossible to take seriously anymore. It's like asking a composer where he finds all those great melodies. But it's a fair question to ask, obvious or no; an idea is where all creative endeavors begin, so why wouldn't an investigation into the process start there?

Most people, I think, ask the question hoping to find out where writers look for inspiration; newspapers, movies, Craigslist personals? But some are really asking another question altogether, which is: How in God's name do we find the needle of a great story idea in the mountainous haystack of sight and sound that is everyday experience?

And my answer to that question is, "We just do." It's like this:

A Non-Writer and a Writer are walking down the street. Both take note of a mismatched pair of running shoes dangling from their bound laces over the back of a vacant bus bench.

The Non-Writer thinks:

"Hmm. That's funny. I wonder what that's all about?" The Writer thinks:

"An all-clear sign left by one criminal conspirator for another."

"A poor man training for his last marathon before cancer takes his life has just boarded a bus and left his only pair of running shoes behind."

"Throwing his worthless ass out again, a grifter's wife has chucked all his clothes and personal belongings out the window of their fourth-floor apartment, starting with shoes she's been careful to tie up in mismatched pairs just to twist the knife."

You see? And none of this is particularly deliberate. It just happens. It's how our minds work. We see or read something that piques our curiosity and runaway extrapolation occurs. Mind you, it isn't always great extrapolation (as the three examples above probably indicate), but every now and then, something genuinely wonderful results from it.

So where do I get my ideas? Everywhere. The thing is, they're only "ideas" because, as a writer, I'm able to perceive them as such; what the Non-Writer dismisses as mere oddities I latch onto as seedlings that could grow stories in a hundred different directions.

Go figure.

My Writing Process

Once I have an idea that so excites me I can't do anything but develop it into a novel, I usually just jump in, sans outline, and let the writing take me where it will. Characters and plot lines fall naturally into place as I go, everything in perfect order ... until I'm inevitably forced to stop, step away from the laptop, and admit that I'll never escape the impenetrable gulag I've imprisoned myself in if I don't draw myself a little map, showing the way out. So I do.

This last part can be fun, but it generally isn't. In fact, I'd compare it to putting a puzzle together without the aid of the picture on the box. Patience and a lot of trial and error are most definitely required.

And there you have it. Gar Anthony Haywood's unique take on the Creative Process. I could go on and on describing it, laying it all out for you like the blueprints to the Kingdom of Heaven, but Tim's not paying me a dime for this piece and there might be a bestselling e-book in the material somewhere down the line. So I'll just sign off for now and leave you wanting for more.

I believe that's the "Dan Brown" method of writing.

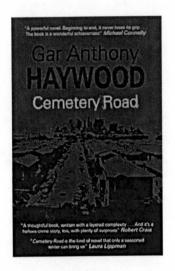

Excerpt

Cemetery Road

by

Gar Anthony Haywood

One of life's greatest mercies is the impermanence of memory.

Some memories lose their shape and form faster than others. Details dim and disappear, forever out of reach of the conscious mind. Settings shift and grow vague, while the people in them perform all nature of tricks, morphing into others and moving about at will, either imposing themselves upon a time and place in which they played no part, or vacating one that holds little meaning without them. Six men in a room become two, three become five. The variations are endless.

Other memories, meanwhile, prove themselves to be indelible.

The smile of an old girlfriend; the sound of a car crash; the pain of a knife wound at the very instant the blade invades your flesh.

For me, it has always been a voice.

It is the voice of a child. Small, female, infused with dread. When she comes to me in my sleep, she never utters more than a single word, yet the inflection she places upon it is something I have been unable to shake for going on three decades:

Daddy.

It is a plea for mercy not intended for me. I am not the child's father. But I am the only one there to hear her, and to see the flames of a raging fire threatening to engulf her, so I am the one she is left to implore.

Her name is Sienna.

She has fair skin and dark brown hair that radiates in curls around her face like silken ribbon. Her eyes are wide, the color of a golden sunset, and her cheeks are aglow with youth and untested innocence. She is the most beautiful black child I have ever seen, and she is only three years old.

Daddy, she says.

She is not my responsibility. I have never laid eyes on her before, and her father is all but a stranger to me. If I reach out to save her, I am as doomed as she, because the fire is not the only danger such an act will require me to face. I know this, and I am paralyzed by the thought. But I eventually go to her nonetheless, diving into the white hot halo surrounding her with arms outstretched, fingers beckoning.

Then, suddenly, smoke floods my lungs and fills my eyes, and the girl is no longer there to be rescued. I am alone in the fire, and it has me in its full and immutable grasp before I can even open my mouth to scream.

It is all a false memory, of course. The fire is of my own invention.

Still, even with my eyes wide open, I can sometimes feel its tendrils peeling the flesh off my bones just the same.

About Gar Anthony Haywood

Gar Anthony Haywood is the Shamus and Anthony Award-winning author of twelve crime novels, including two standalone thrillers written under the pen name Ray Shannon. His short fiction has been included in the *Best American Mystery Stories* anthologies, and *VIBE* magazine once identified his first novel, *Fear of the Dark*, as essential reading for those looking to "widen (their) eyes to a multicultural reality." His most recent novel is *Cemetery Road*. The six books in his Aaron Gunner P.I. Series, beginning with *Fear of the Dark* and *Not Long for This World*, have just been re-issued as e-books by Mysterious Press.

Wendy Hornsby

"Hornsby has created a true heroine for our times – a professional woman who is intelligent, feminine but tough, clever without resorting to cuteness and as resourceful as a Navy SEAL with a Swiss Army knife. Long may she survive."

—Dick Lochte, *LA Times*

I was a Wendy Hornsby fan before I met her, and the primary reason I was a fan was the character whom writer/critic Dick Lochte describes above, a documentary filmmaker named Maggie MacGowen. Maggie, the heroine of Hornsby's remarkable mystery series, is intelligent, passionate, resourceful, entertaining—everything you'd want in someone you're going to spend 300 pages with. And she's not the only great character in the books. Edgar- winner S.J. Rozan sums it up: "The joy of Wendy Hornsby's books has always been as much her characters and the relationships among them as the story itself."

And, oh, yeah, the stories themselves. They're models of character-driven mysteries, which is to say that they're full-blown novels about three-dimensional people confronting crises in their lives, and somewhere in there is a full-fledged, intricate mystery that the greats of the Golden Age would have been proud to claim. So it was kind of a relief to me to read Wendy's essay and learn that her books are hard to write. It wouldn't be fair otherwise.

Plotter, Pantser, Plodder

Plotter, pantser and plodder, I am all three at some point during the process of writing a book, but certainly more a pantser than a plotter.

Years ago, I took a seminar with English author P.D. James. She described for us how, before she began to write a book, she first built a very complex story outline that she would hang on a wall. Having planned the entire book, she would write individual scenes—by hand—out of sequence and then hang them on that outline, something like decorating a Christmas tree. I confess that I was agog. Obviously, that system works for her; her novels are dense, complex, orderly, and lovely.

Writing is a very idiosyncratic process. What works for her doesn't work for me. I gave Dame Phyllis' system a shot, but kept pruning and rearranging that written outline as my story evolved until that original outline tree looked more like a bonsai on hormones than a well-shaped Tannenbaum.

Way back in the pre-PC olden days, when I wrote on an electric typewriter, I carefully outlined and pondered and plotted before I typed every word because it was such a pain to retype pages when I made changes or mistakes. Think about Mark Twain writing by hand with a steel-tip pen; he wrote *Huckleberry Finn* in one draft—wouldn't you?

But then I acquired a computer and began to compose directly on the keyboard, a system that, with the help of flat surfaces for sticky notes, suits my method of constantly writing and rewriting a story as it emerges just fine.

By the time I acquired my first PC I had also acquired two active children, a college teaching position and a household to run. There was a Day Planner floating around that listed the day's target events, but getting everything accomplished meant a constant shuffling and reshuffling of available resources; the day remained fluid around a structural core of

work and school until it was time for lights out
involve duplicating a midterm, taking anoth
carpool to soccer practice because she had the
orthodontist, remembering to take something
for dinner, de-worming the cat, picking up car
overseeing homework, preparing dinner, teachir
gaps—waiting at traffic lights, sitting in the ortl
spaghetti—I kept reworking the plot of whatever book was in process so
that, once the household had settled in for the night, I could sit down and
efficiently write. Somehow, it all worked out.

The kids are grown and on their own, and doing just fine, thank you; I
still teach. Though there are fewer distractions now, I still have plenty to
juggle and I still write in essentially the same way.

Do I plot before I write? Sure, in my head and on sticky notes. But the
way that plot unfolds remains fluid until I return the copy-edited proofs.
That is, until the book goes to the printer. The only time I create anything
that looks like a written outline is when it's time for a new contract. I send
my editor a pithy paragraph or two and a sketchy outline for the rest of
the story as I see it before I begin serious writing.

But after that, for me, making too many plans for well-developed
characters and the story that they drive is something like making strong-
willed children eat anything green: I can put broccoli in front of them, but
if they won't eat broccoli, they won't eat broccoli. (I won't either, by the
way, so don't ask me why I chose that as an example.)

Don't take this to mean that I write in a sort of free fall. My process is
more like jazz: first I build an internal structure around setting and
character and the crime that will be crux of the story, and then I
improvise.

The origin of the story itself comes out of the ether. I will read or see
something, go somewhere, hear something, and for who knows what
reason that event or situation begins to build within a story in my
imagination. If I find that event or situation to be compelling enough, I'll
do some research. I surf the Internet, walk the ground where the story
would take place, talk to people, take notes, take pictures, go to the
library. Now people move into the story and begin to carry it, to act. I can
hear their voices, begin to know their histories. At that point, if I am still

ow there will be a book or a short story and I begin giving
o what had been random scenes and ideas.

ause my books are mysteries, I know that a crime of some sort will
entral to all action. The nature of the crime determines the scope of the
story and sets its pace: looking for a lost puppy leaves time to stop for tea
now and then; saving the world from nuclear winter does not.

The setting of the book determines the tone of the book, the sorts of
characters that will populate the book, and the sort of crime that would
upset their world.

My last three books were set—in this order—in the barrios of Los
Angeles (*In the Guise of Mercy*), in rural Normandy (*The Paramour's
Daughter*), and on a college campus (*The Hanging*). Though they are all
stories that feature my series character, Maggie MacGowen, the crimes
and the people in those stories differ a great deal as I tailored them to suit
their milieux. (After ten books together, I have a fairly good handle on
Maggie MacGowen and her continuing cast of friends, but I am still
frequently surprised by what they do.)

Long before I get to the point of writing that sketch for my editor, I will
know the story's essentials: what happened to upset the order of society,
what impact that event will have and on whom, and how order will be
restored.

For the rest, I fly by the seat of my pants.

Excerpt

The Hanging

by

Wendy Hornsby

"They're here to arrest me, aren't they?"

"They won't do anything until after the funeral," I said, stealing a glance toward the college gym's exit doors where Detectives Thornbury and Weber stood, feet shoulder-width apart like soldiers at parade rest, unmoving yet seeing everything and everyone in the room.

Uncle Max reached forward from his seat behind us and clamped a hand on Sly's shoulder as a reminder for him to keep his mouth shut.

Sly dropped his head and wiped his hands on his pants legs before he clenched them together. He was as thin as a splinter, but compared to the scrawny urchin I had pulled in off the streets a decade earlier, he was downright robust; I thought he looked handsome in his new blue suit.

A lot of people in that room were keeping an eye on Sly. The course of life is rarely a straightaway; his certainly had not been. But it seemed to me that he was handling the curves recently thrown at him with grace.

I looked around, checking on Guido's film crew, camera placements and lights, caught his eye and got a nod that meant all was well. The cameras were fairly unobtrusive, but they were a presence just the same. As I turned back around, I saw that Detective Thornbury was staring at me.

I leaned in close to Sly and whispered. "Don't worry, kid, if they put you in the slam, I'll bake you a cake."

He slid his eyes toward me and managed a smile. "Promise, Maggie?"

"Promise," I said.

"What kind?"

"What else? Devil's food."

Uncle Max cleared his throat, a signal for me to shut up as well.

Sly mouthed, You okay? I nodded, gave his arm a squeeze, mouthed, You? He smiled gamely.

The big gymnasium doors swung open and six men, all of them wearing dark suits, all members of the college administration except for handsome Trey Holloway, the dead man's son, wheeled the mahogany coffin in out of the rain.

I saw the basketball coach scowl. I don't know how Coach felt about Park Holloway, but it was basketball season and Coach had protested mightily against holding the memorial service for Holloway in his gym. But it was still raining heavily, predicted to continue into the afternoon, and with the auditorium closed for earthquake retrofitting there was no other indoor space on campus large enough to contain the five- or six-hundred members of the campus community who had come to pay their last respects to the murdered man.

As the coffin came down the center aisle the crowd stood as they would for a bride and watched the mortuary trolley progress toward the out-of-bounds line where a priest, a rabbi, a Buddhist monk, a Methodist preacher and a Chumash Indian shaman waited in front of a bank of potted palms and Easter lilies. That line up of men dressed in their various forms of clerical garb would certainly be fodder for corny jokes once this collegiate congregation was sprung. A priest, a rabbi, a monk, a preacher and a shaman walked into a bar....

Lew Kaufman leaned across Sly after the coffin passed us and whispered. "Damn, Maggie, I was hoping for an open coffin. You know, just to make sure the bastard's dead."

About Wendy Hornsby

Published internationally, Edgar Award winning author Wendy Hornsby is the author of ten novels and many short stories. Critics have described Wendy's mysteries as "refreshing, real, and raunchy" (*NY Times*), "unusually poignant" (*LA Times*), and "powerful writing and... equally thought-provoking story" (*Publisher's Weekly*).

The Hanging (Perseverance Press, forthcoming September 2012), is the latest in her award-winning Maggie MacGowen series, and follows *In the Guise of Mercy* (Perseverance Press, 2009) and *The Paramour's Daughter* (Perseverance Press, 2010 see www.danielpublishing.com), both of which are available in Kindle editions. Wendy's first seven titles, including *Telling Lies, Midnight Baby, Bad Intent, 77th Street Requiem* and *A Hard Light*, are now available on Kindle from www.MysteriousPress.com. Wendy, a Professor of History, lives with her husband in Southern California. For further information about the author and her work, go to her website: www.wendyhornsby.com.

Debbi Mack

"Debbi Mack has carved her own niche in the mystery pantheon."

—Bestselling author Scott Nicholson

Debbi Mack is that most modern of writers, an ebook bestseller. (A New York Times *besteller, no less.)*

Ahh, ebooks. If you talk to traditional publishers, many will suggest that ebooks are the end of civilization as we know it. If you talk to writers, thousands and thousands of them will tell you that the ebook is the greatest thing to happen to literature since the invention of ink. It makes writing democratic. It opens wide the gates of genre, commercial appeal, and even quality, that previously limited what books reach us. It breaks the stranglehold over what we read that was exerted for so long by a relatively small number of people in a few blocks of (mostly midtown) Manhattan.

And here's what else it is. It's a brutally difficult arena to succeed in. Nowhere is the signal-to-noise ratio greater and harder to battle. Hundreds of thousands of ebooks come out every month. Many of them are dreadful and a few of them are extraordinary. Debbi Mack has won distinction at the "extraordinary" end of the spectrum as a thriller writer of wit, verve, and inventiveness whose protagonist, lawyer Sam McRae, would be a bestseller in any format.

Dr. Strange Writer:
or How I Learned Stop Relying on Outlines and Just Let Go

I'm a planner and organizer by nature, so when I write a novel, I always start with an outline. I've never used a terribly detailed outline, because that would be tantamount to writing the book in miniature and where's the fun in that? However, in order to write a mystery, I need a sense of where I'm going and who did the deed, so I can plant clues and red herrings while building a plot big enough to tell the whole story. Thus, the outline creates a roadmap that leads my protagonist from the inciting event that compels her to investigate the mystery through a series of events that include major turning points where key information is revealed (or not), which lead up to the climax and conclusion where the plot threads come together, she solves the mystery and justice is served (one way or the other).

When I started writing fiction, my outlines were generally structured in three acts, in the manner of Syd Field's advice in the book *Screenplay*. Since then, I've read more about story structure and experimented with various storytelling methods.

Among the most helpful books I've read on the subject are Carolyn Wheat's *How to Write Killer Fiction*. This book suggests telling the story in four parts, an approach that boils down to a simple variation on the basic three-act structure.

Another great book about story structure is Blake Edward's *Save the Cat*. This makes two books about screenwriting that I've looked to for inspiration in my novel writing. Great films start with well-written screenplays. I believe the best way to write a great novel is to get down to business and tell a great story.

It was while studying screenwriting that I lea
storytelling structure called "The Hero's Journey." Thi
follow now, when I outline. It's a 12-step structure. It sou
but it isn't really. Basically, you could see it as three
divided into four parts or vice versa.

One way to break down "The Hero's Journey," synthesized by
mythologist Joseph Campbell, is as follows: (1) The Ordinary World—The
hero's world before the challenge begins; (2) Call to Adventure—The hero
is presented with the problem or challenge; (3) Refusal of the Call—The
hero is reluctant to accept the challenge; (4) Meeting the Mentor—The
hero encounters a guide or adviser; (5) Crossing the Threshold—
Committed, the hero enters the world of the adventure; (6) Tests, Allies,
Enemies—The hero meets challenges and encounters friends and enemies;
(7) Approach—Meeting setbacks, the hero may have to plan a new way
forward; (8) Ordeal—The biggest crisis; everything on the line; (9)
Reward—The hero survives and is apparently victorious; (10) The Road
Back—Return to the ordinary world; (11) Resurrection Hero—A last test
in which the hero faces death or final defeat; (12) Return with "Elixir"—
The hero returns again to the ordinary world, with solution(s) in hand.

While this twelve-stage progression is the time-tested method of telling
mythic stories of heroic quests, when you come down to it, good
storytelling always seems to boil down to the basic Aristotelian three-act
structure, one way or another. The question is whether you plan it or do it
on the fly.

As I explained, I tend to be a planner. However, not everything about a
novel can be planned in advance. I've learned this in the process of
writing several novels, some of which remain unpublished.

My outlines are always very general and allow room for me to make
changes as needed, as the characters or situation demand. However, even
as I make changes, I do so with the ultimate goal of revealing the killer in
the back of my mind. And this is how my outline keeps my story on
course, while allowing the characters and situation to add elements that
come as a surprise to me.

When I started writing fiction, I usually had a pretty good idea what I
wanted my characters to do and why, even though I didn't spell out
exactly when or how in advance. As a writer, it gave me a sense of

..ort that I knew where I was going with the story by outlining the
are bones and having some idea of what the characters were going to do
beforehand.

As I've written more books, I've noticed the characters taking on a life
of their own and telling me what they want to do. I've learned that I need
to listen to them and not simply manipulate them like puppets. This
means I can't plan the entire plot in advance. I need to trust the characters
to tell me what they want and why. I do this with the knowledge of where
they're probably going to end up eventually and what their underlying
motivations are. However, that doesn't mean I have to plan each and
every thing they do in advance of writing the story, nor do I want to,
anymore.

I've continued to use The Hero's Journey outline, but only to
determine the very bare bones plot points of the story.

My approach to storytelling is now best described as a hybrid between
outlining and writing it on the fly. I still use an outline for structure, but I
feel free to explore where the characters want to go between the plot
points.

I'm much more open to listening to what the characters are saying,
writing it down, and seeing where it goes. I still have my goal squarely in
mind. It's just a matter of how I get there, and I feel free to let the
characters tell me what they want instead of manipulating them.

I liken this to a continuing dialogue between my characters and myself.
I guess this is what authors mean when they say, "My characters talk to
me." I also think this represents what writers refer to as learning to trust
the process.

By doing this, I find the story can go places I couldn't have imagined
when I first outlined the idea. As a result, the plot can include twists or
other elements that come as a surprise even to me.

I've learned that in writing, as in life, sometimes you simply have to let
go and hope for the best. And that's when the most miraculous things can
happen. In your writing and in your life.

Excerpt

Riptide

by

Debbi Mack

The pounding woke me. I felt for the bedside lamp, turned it on, and looked around the unfamiliar room.

The swimsuit flung onto the broken wicker chair told me I was in the right place.

My best friend Jamila and I had rented the condo for a week, a gift to ourselves before pressing flesh at the annual bar association convention in Ocean City, Maryland…

More pounding. The noise came from the front door. I glanced at the bedside clock. 1:35 A.M. What the fuck?

The banging resumed. I rolled out of bed, trudged to the door and opened it. Jamila stood in the short hall between our rooms. She held a creamy white bathrobe closed across her sizeable chest.

Jamila looked amazing for someone who'd been startled out of bed in the wee hours. Despite pillow-tousled hair and sleepy eyes, she was a dusky Queen of Sheba in figure-revealing silk to my anemic court jester in striped men's pajamas.

"Who on earth could that be, Sam?" Jamila hissed.

"I don't know." My words were stupid and obvious.

Another round of pounding. I moved to the door and peered through the peephole, before our visitor pounded his knuckles bloody.

On the other side stood a uniformed cop. Sighing, I opened the door.

"Good evening, ma'am," the cop said.

"Good morning, you mean." Wail on my door in the middle of the night and you're guaranteed an audience with the Wicked Witch of the West.

The cop took a step back then recovered quickly. "Sorry to wake you at this hour—" he started.

I cut him off. "Please tell me this doesn't have to do with our friends on the first floor. I thought we had that straightened out."

"No ma'am. This is far more serious."

It better be. And quit calling me ma'am. I heard Jamila shuffle up behind me.

A female officer moved into view. She consulted a notepad. "Are you Stephanie Ann McRae?" she asked.

"Right. What's this about?"

The woman ignored me. "And you're Jamila Williams?"

"Yes." Jamila sounded tired, unsure. She moved closer.

"Is this yours, Ms. Williams?" The man held up a plastic bag containing a decorative tortoise shell comb. The four-pronged, fan-shaped comb was distinctively marbled.

Jamila blinked. "Can I see that?"

He handed it to her for inspection.

"It... looks like one of mine," she said. "One that I lost. Where did you find this?"

The cops exchanged a look.

"I'm sorry, ma'am, but you need to come with us."

"What?" I said. "What the hell is this?"

"Ms. Williams, we need to take you in for questioning."

Adrenaline pumped through me, bringing me to full alert. "Questioning?" My voice was shrill. "What's going on?"

"William Raymond Wesley has been murdered. We just need to ask you a few questions at the station."

The man droned on. The night had turned surreal. I tried to get more specifics, but Jamila silenced me with a raised hand. Probably didn't want to look uncooperative. Reluctantly, I backed down.

Everyone seemed to move in slow motion. The woman escorted Jamila to her room so she could get dressed.

Who the hell is William Raymond Wesley? Then, I remembered.

Jamila emerged in a warm-up suit. With a firm hand on Jamila's arm, the female cop escorted her while holding onto an evidence bag with her pajamas and robe. Jamila and I exchanged a look that said she, too, recalled how we'd met the victim.

About Debbi Mack

Debbi Mack is the *New York Times* ebook bestselling author of the Sam McRae mystery series. Her latest novel, *Riptide*, is available on Amazon, Amazon UK, Barnes & Noble and Smashwords as are the previous books in the series, *Identity Crisis* and *Least Wanted*. She's also published *Five Uneasy Pieces*, a short story collection that includes her Derringer Award–nominated story "The Right to Remain Silent." Her short stories have appeared in various anthologies and publications, including *Shaken: Stories for Japan*, an anthology created to benefit Japanese tsunami relief efforts. That anthology is also available on Amazon UK.

A former attorney, Debbi has also worked as a journalist, reference librarian, and freelance writer/researcher. She's currently working on a young adult novel, planning Sam's next adventure, and generally mulling over other projects. You can find her online at her website, where she publishes a monthly column. She also has five blogs, including My Life on the Midlist, The Book Grrl and Random and Sundry Things. You can find her on Facebook and Twitter.

Mike Orenduff

"...funny at a very high intellectual level and deliciously delightful."

—*The Baltimore Sun*

Mike Orenduff's books are simultaneously classic and original. They're classic in the sense that they present mysteries that obey the dictates of the Golden Age: a murder or murders, not too much gore on the page, a nicely contained nest of suspects, clues more or less in plain sight (if you're very good at spotting them). And original *in the sense that he's invented a unique character—a pot thief, at least according to the U.S. Government rules that define anyone who finds and digs up a Native American pot as a thief. And then Orenduff has married that thief, and his vivid New Mexico setting, to a different piece of classical historical erudition in each book. Thus, we have The Pot Thief Who Studied Pythagoras, or Ptolemy or Einstein or Escoffier or D.H. Lawrence.*

The Escoffier book immortalizes the worst idea for a fictional restaurant I've ever read, Mexican/Austrian fusion. But the restaurant works, just as improbably and as successfully as this fusion of classical authors with New Mexico murder works, and it works largely because Hubert (Hubie) Schuze, Orenduff's pot thief, is just one member of a cast of memorable, highly individual characters, and because Orenduff is an extremely funny writer and a truly nimble plotter. And maybe that's why his books have won a pot full of prizes.

A Story Is Someone Doing Something

Forty years later, the setting remains vivid. A desk with a typewriter, a felt-tip pen and ten stacks of Post-It notepads, each stack a different color. I don't know how many individual stickies I started with. A thousand or so were on the wall. Probably ten times that many had been up there before being crumpled and discarded. A Partially Truth-Functional System of Modal Logic was being converted from a wall of Post-It notes to typed pages. Each color represented a topic. The columns linked logicians, earliest at the top, from Aristotle (d. 322 B.C.) to C. I. Lewis (d. 1964 A.D.). The rows were my chapters. Of course not every logician dealt with every topic and not every chapter dealt with every topic, so the wall looked like a paint chip display at Sherwin-Williams arranged by a colorblind clerk. But that dissertation earned me a doctorate.

It seems to me that novels plotted in minute detail would read like dissertations – clear, organized and drop-dead boring. But some obsessive plotters turn out fanciful stories with the lyricism of troubadours. I don't understand how they do it. I don't understand why they do it. They will never know the exhilaration of discovering something in your story you didn't anticipate. When I mention this in talks at bookstores and libraries, someone usually asks, "How can you discover something you didn't know? After all, it's your story."

No, it isn't.

I don't write about me. I write about a guy named Hubert Schuze. It's his story. And even though I know him as well as I know my real friends, he sometimes – like those real friends – does things that surprise me.

Telling you how I write a book may help explain this. Stories are not about science, romance, murder or history. They are about people. A story is someone doing something. A good story is an interesting someone doing an interesting something.

Before starting my first Pot Thief book, I wrote Hubie's biography. It wasn't particularly well-written; I wasn't planning to publish it. But it was complete. It contained not only the data of his life (date of birth, parents, schooling, etc.) but, like any good biography, it also dealt with his character—his beliefs, fears, aspirations, values, weaknesses and talents. I made him a person I'd like to hang out with because I was planning to do just that.

I start each book with eight compass points: Who is murdered? Why? How? By whom? How is the murder connected to Hubie's life? How is the murder connected to Hubie's strengths and weaknesses? What is one of the clues? Who is he studying?

The first six are the building blocks of all murder mysteries. I don't know why I want one clue before I start. Perhaps it's a tip of the hat to the plotters. More likely, it is just a warming-up exercise for my sluggish imagination.

Of course I need to know who Hubie is studying in order to have a title. But the real reason I have him reading someone like Einstein is because it gives me a source of ideas.

So let's see how this works in practice. I started the most recent book with the "how" question. I thought it would be interesting if someone were poisoned by one of Hubie's glazing chemicals. That led to the victim question. I decided Hubie would be making plates for a restaurant, and one of the diners would be poisoned. But that doesn't work because once a plate is glazed, you can't absorb the chemical. I wanted to keep the restaurant setting because of Hubie's fascination with food and drink, so I decided to make the victim one of the cooks. Naturally, Hubie would have to study Escoffier. When I did my research, reading everything by and about Escoffier I could find, I discovered that in addition to being a famous chef, he was also an embezzler. So I put Hubie – who already had a background in accounting – into a situation where he would be accused of embezzling from the restaurant. The one clue was one of the characters mistakenly saying *los manos* instead of *las manos*. Don't ask.

The previous paragraph—177 words—was all I needed to start the book. More importantly, it's all I wanted. I wanted to wend my way up the mountain to the climax, not ride to it on a funicular.

I didn't know exactly what things would happen or in what order. I started writing to find out.

A cook named Jürgen was slated to be the victim, but Hubie changed that. After a night of drinking, they have this exchange:

> Jürgen said, "I'm afraid you'll have to take me home."
>
> "I've had too much champagne to be your designated driver."
>
> "Then give me the keys to your vehicle."
>
> "Jürgen, there is no way I will allow you to drive my vehicle in your condition."
>
> He gave me a hurt look. "I'm not going to drive it. I'm going to sleep in it."
>
> "The back window is open. Be my guest."

The next chapter starts:

> Parking garages unnerve me. Their sterile concrete environment almost invites ambush. There being no place to hide seems to apply only to the victim.
>
> The early morning sun shown between the ramps, casting long shadows of the pillars and creating regions of pitch dark.
>
> I approached the Bronco warily. The back window was down as I had left it, and I was happy to see Jürgen's motionless form between the tailgate and the back seat. I reached in to poke him awake then hesitated.
>
> During the night, he had lost about eighty pounds, and his hair had turned from black to brown.
>
> When reason took over, I realized the body in the Bronco was not Jürgen. Then I realized it was indeed a body.

I don't know how I knew that, but I couldn't have been more certain of it had he sported a toe tag and been under a white sheet in the morgue. It wasn't the bump on his head – that didn't look bad enough to be fatal.

Maybe I sensed there was no rise and fall of his chest as he breathed. Maybe it was his unnaturally awkward position. Maybe it was his pallor. The skin on the back of his neck had a bluish grey tinge. In the cold night air of Santa Fe's 7200 feet, he had dropped considerably below 98.6 degrees. He was not so cold that you could use him to ice down a bottle of Gruet, but neither was he room temperature.

I stood there debating whether to touch him. If by some miracle he were alive, I didn't want him to die because I failed to seek help. So despite the fact that I was positive he was dead, and despite the fact that I hated the idea of touching a dead person, I placed my hand on his shoulder and shoved him.

"Barry?" I said.

He didn't answer. I touched his neck. It was even colder than it looked. I went back to my room and called 911. Then I sat there wondering how a live Jürgen Dorfmeister had become a dead Barry Stiles in the back of my Bronco in the parking garage of the La Fonda.

The sentence, "During the night, he had lost about eighty pounds, and his hair had turned from black to brown" came out of nowhere. It's exactly the way Hubie would phrase it. I know I hit the keys that made the letters appear, but it was Hubie, his knack for being in odd situations and his quirky way of seeing things that made that sentence appear. And it saved Jürgen and killed poor Barry in the prime of his life.

Try planning that in advance, plotters.

Excerpt

The Pot Thief Who Studied Escoffier

by

Mike Orenduff

"I can't believe this is happening to me."

"It's the restaurant syndrome, Hubie."

"Restaurant syndrome? I've never heard of it."

"Maybe you know it by its original name, *le syndrome de restaurant*."

I groaned. "Please, no more French words and phrases."

"But that's it. That's the syndrome. You start working in a restaurant, and you have to learn all those French terms. It begins to affect your thinking, like the twins thing."

"The twins thing?"

"Yeah. You know, like how twins have this special language that makes it easy for them to communicate with each other, but it messes them up when they try to deal with normal people. Restaurant workers are like that. We may start out normal, but after you begin using words like *prix fixe, hors-d'œuvres, à la carte, escargots,* and *raison d'être,* you get a little crazy."

"*Raison d'être?*"

"I think it's a raisin soufflé."

"No. I think the phrase for a raisin soufflé is *au courant*," I said.

"Anyway," she continued, "it affects your judgment, and pretty soon you're doing crazy things like actually eating snails because you think of them as *escargots* and don't realize they're just slimy snails. And the next thing you know, you're funneling money from the restaurant to your personal account."

"I didn't 'funnel money'. I was just trying to keep the place in business."

"I could see the changes come over you, Hubie. I noticed it when you called me up there to waitress. You weren't yourself. Taking charge, showing leadership, inventing dishes."

"Thanks a lot."

She laughed. "Admit it, that is not exactly you."

"You're right. But I really invented only one dish, the *Schnitzel con tres chiles*. Rafael invented all three appetizers. Even Miss Gladys contributed with *Tafelspitz Sangre de Cristo*."

"I can't imagine what Alain thought about that one."

"He said it had a certain *Je ne sais quoi*."

"See. There you go again with the French. I hear that all the time, Hubie. What does it mean?"

"I don't know what."

"Really? I thought you would know."

"I do know. It means I don't know what."

"If you don't know what, how can you say you know what it means?"

I raised my glass. "*To le syndrome de restaurant*."

About Mike Orenduff

Mike Orenduff grew up in a house so close to the Rio Grande that he could Frisbee a tortilla into Mexico. While in graduate school at the

University of New Mexico, he worked during the summer as a volunteer teacher at one of the nearby pueblos. After receiving his M.A. at New Mexico and his Ph.D. at Tulane, he became a university professor. He went on to serve as President of New Mexico State University. After retiring from higher education, he began writing his award-winning Pot Thief murder mysteries which combine archaeology and philosophy with humor and mystery. Among his many awards are the "Lefty" national award for best humorous mystery, two "Eppies" for the best ebook mysteries and the New Mexico Book of the Year Award.

His books have been described by The El Paso Times as "the perfect fusion of murder, mayhem and margaritas."

The Pot Thief Who Studied Pythagoras, The Pot Thief Who Studied Ptolemy, The Pot Thief Who Studied Einstein, The Pot Thief Who Studied Escoffier and The Pot Thief Who Studied D. H. Lawrence are available in paper from independent bookshops as well as from Amazon and Barnes & Noble. E-book versions are available on Kindle. Signed copies are available from the author: ThePotThief@gmail.com

The 6th book in the series, The Pot Thief Who Studied Billy the Kid, is forthcoming in late 2012.

Stephen Jay Schwartz

"Just as I thought there wasn't an original take left on the detective novel, along comes Stephen Jay Schwartz and *Beat*."

—*New York Times* best-selling author Michael Connelly

Stephen Jay Schwartz, it seems to me, is as much a poet as a thriller writer. I don't know of many writers whose prose sings in such a distinctive voice, nor do many writers whom I know personally take such extraordinary pains over virtually every word on the page. And, perhaps most remarkably, by the time Stephen is finally finished with a sentence, or a paragraph, or a chapter, all that work is buried beneath the sheer pace and vision of his writing.

His fictional world is full of flawed people, some of whom are struggling to be whole. Boulevard *and* Beat *have the heightened intensity of fever dreams. I sometimes think of them as full-color noir, if that's not a contradiction in terms. They're not always for the faint-hearted reader, but for those with a high tolerance for human frailty and high-voltage action, they're required reading. (And he's a former screenwriter, so we have another outliner!)*

I'll Take a Road Map, Thank You Very Much

I spent years writing feature screenplays before leaping into *Boulevard*, my first novel. Screenplays are nothing if not plot. Structure is king and there's simply no room for fat.

Screenwriters are used to writing very detailed outlines and treatments before tackling their assignments. A treatment is a short story version of the film, with one paragraph of description for every scene in the movie. The treatments I write for screenplays usually run between fifteen and twenty-five pages, single-spaced.

I wanted a different experience when it came to writing my first novel. I wanted to jump right in—no outline, no treatment—and wallow in the magic. And I did, and it was incredibly freeing. Characters and situations seemed to download into my mind from a universal, collective unconscious, and the plot points and character arcs evolved organically. It was wonderful. Until I wrote myself into a corner. Until I got stuck.

I had too much information swimming in my head. I couldn't effectively foreshadow and play off my plot points because I had no perspective on the story as a whole. I was lost in the tangents. My characters were coming to life, but they were wandering, tripping over themselves. I needed an outline.

As I wrote the outline I felt compelled to include more detail. And so the outline became a treatment. And I realized I preferred it that way.

Some authors find this process boring.

I feel exactly the opposite. The detailed outline actually frees me to explore the scene when I finally sit down to write it. The treatment provides guideposts that anchor it, giving me the room to tinker with character motivation while remaining confident that I won't take the story on a hundred-page tangent. I let the characters be themselves and say what they need to say and often, very often, I'm surprised by what comes out. Sometimes they actually change the direction of the scene, which results in a change in the direction of the story from that point forward.

(Or backward, if I have to go back and "fix" story points to accommodate the new material). If the change feels good, I adjust my outline or treatment as well, so that I have an updated "road map" for the ever-evolving novel.

When I was writing *Beat*, my second novel, I again tried to break from the outline. I knew that many authors wrote by the "seat of their pants" and I was determined to find my way into their process. Soon, however, I found myself completely and unbearably lost. I ended up throwing out ninety hard-fought pages. It was terribly frustrating. I decided to go "old school" and bought a pack of 3 X 5 cards. I wrote brief scene ideas on the cards and posted them onto a large, pushpin board. With the cards on the board I had a birds-eye view of the plot. I moved some of the cards around, combined others, threw a handful away. When I was happy with the bare-bones structure I went back to the computer and listed the scenes in order, creating a bare-bones outline for the plot. From there I filled in the blanks and wrote a very detailed treatment. Only then did I know the story would work.

Another element I incorporated was colored text. I used black text to tell the story, red text to highlight very important moments, and blue text to indicate aspects of the plot that I knew, but didn't want the reader to know until later in the story. This way I had a clear picture of what I intended to hide or reveal at any given point.

This process allowed me to see the entire canvas—beginning/middle/end—in a glance, with every subtle brushstroke in-between. I had the freedom to explore within the scene, and I discovered that much of the exposition I had "front-loaded" into scenes in my earlier draft could instead be drawn out over the course of seven or eight scenes, and a lot of it could be eliminated entirely. It gave me perspective.

It also gave me the freedom to explore quirky character traits and minor character sub-plots, knowing they would work in conjunction with the more important expositional beats I'd already plotted. Knowing they wouldn't slow the story's momentum.

Once I saw that the story worked on paper, I felt a tremendous sense of relief. I was on deadline for my second novel and I didn't have time to write and rewrite the book, over and over again, the way I did with my first novel. I spent 3 ½ years writing *Boulevard*, and I was contracted to write the sequel in about a year. I spent six months of that time getting lost in the magic of research, and another two months writing myself into corners, before deciding to fully jump on the outline bandwagon. With the outline and treatment done, I was able to write the novel in less than two months.

Still, I believe the process benefits from different approaches, depending on how much time I have and what the particular story requires. I like to do some "seat-of-the-pants" writing early on, as an exercise to help me discover the story's central motifs. To bring character back-story to life. To determine whether this is a story that absolutely needs to be told. But when the scenes start piling up, I get them into an outline as soon as possible.

My general observation is that authors who come from film and TV are plotters—they write outlines or treatments before writing their books. Film and television writing often requires the writer to "pitch" a fully-realized story before he is awarded a writing assignment. The screenwriter also faces the "development room," where producers, development executives, film directors, studio executives and various assistants have a say in how the story will play out.

It behooves the writer to bring his or her vision to these meetings early on, usually in the form of a treatment, in order to maintain some sense of creative control. This is why so many screenwriters flee the film business in favor of writing novels, where they can truly be the author of their works. Some abandon the "plotter's world" entirely, embracing the freedom of writing without following a road map. Others take the screenwriting tools they've forged and adapt them for the challenges of writing novels only.

It all comes down to rewriting. I'm either rewriting the outline and treatment or I'm rewriting the entire novel. A lot of authors write their novels fast and loose and consider the first draft a throw-away. Some authors change character names and genders mid-stream and invent plot-lines that materialize out of thin air. It's their process. They clean it up in the second and third drafts. But it kills me to have to toss a whole draft. When I sit down to write that first paragraph I want it to be my very best work. I want it to be as close to a final draft as I can make it. And, after I've labored over every sentence and word, the thought of tossing it makes me want to cry. Sometimes it can't be avoided. But if I've written (and rewritten) a strong outline before starting the process, if I've front-loaded my research and layered it into the treatment, then the writing of that first draft becomes a pleasure. I have all the tools at my disposal.

The bottom line is that I'd much rather kill my outlined scenes or a few pages of the treatment than experience the pain of tossing fully-realized chapters into the trash.

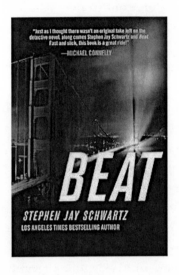

Excerpt

Beat

by

Stephen Jay Schwartz

Hayden turned the corner onto Market Street, and the full force of San Francisco hit him like the gale that swept down from the hills. Scores of homeless pushed past, shoeless, pants soiled from ancient excretions, caked with grease and dirt and the oils that pooled in the driveways and sleepways of back-alley camps. Tweakers like zombies, white and pasty skinned with dark forest eyes and vacant stares. Hip teenage grunge addicts ruined by heroin, obsessively scratching their scalps under black knit skullcaps, scratching their chests and arms for the invisible gnat that tickled needle marks and abscessed scars. Wasted talent—what the narcs called the fifteen-, sixteen-, seventeen-year-old street girls who still had a little blush in their cheeks, who perched nevertheless on the edges of self-made chasms, preparing to take the plunge. Limbless beggars crippled on wooden stilts or sitting forever in ancient rusted wheelchairs, toeing themselves from one storefront to the next, shaking empty 7-Eleven Big Gulp cups in the hope of attracting a handful of nickels and dimes. Pimps, dealers, hookers, petty thieves, hustlers, quick-change artists, pick-pockets, parolees, rapists, murderers. There wasn't a single person on Market Street whose intentions were good.

Hayden waded through the mess of it, pushing forward toward some imagined oasis. He knew San Francisco wasn't that big and if he kept walking, he'd end up someplace he'd rather be. He caught a glimpse of himself in the window of a Walgreens pharmacy. His eyes looked bewildered. Shit, he thought, I fit right in.

His thick dark hair was matted to his scalp from a combination of sweat and blood. The strong lines of his cheekbones and chin were reduced to a soft swollen mush. There were U-shaped black-blue-and-yellow knots on his jaw from where the steel-toed boots had made their marks. From the pain in his ribs and legs, he figured the bruising continued under his clothes. His jacket was torn and soaked with blood, and he realized it came from the bullet hole in his chest. He remembered now that he'd been shot.

He felt an onrush of pain. Waves of nausea. Sweat boiled off his forehead. The people in his path came forward in a blur. Loud voices in his ear, the screaming of madmen, their expressions suddenly challenging him, their mouths stretched to incredible widths.

Then he saw her, not ten feet away. Cora with her long red hair, the gentle sway of her hips, her round, soft shoulders, her air of confidence, her youthful gait.

Hayden pushed his legs to follow her on the street. He kept pace, feeling the strain in his calves and quadriceps as he turned onto Powell Street to encounter the long, steep incline leading up to Nob Hill. The cable car turnaround sat to his left, and thirty tourists stood waiting for a five-dollar ride. He veered clumsily into the group and felt himself pushed back by shoulders and gloved hands. The hill slowed his pace, but it slowed Cora's as well. He stood five steps behind her as they approached Union Square. He reached out as they crossed Geary, but when she turned, it wasn't her. Not even close.

Hayden looked left and right. The thieves and hustlers had been replaced by men in suits and ties. The soup kitchens and SROs had become Macy's and Neiman Marcus and Saks Fifth Avenue. He trudged up the hill, passing the opulent Westin St. Francis and its bellhops in their flamboyant tunics. They stared, challenging him to cross an imaginary line. Hayden veered away, walking the sidewalk edge like a tightrope.

At the sound of gunshots, he dropped and threw himself against a parked car. It stopped as quickly as it had begun, and when the smoke lifted, Hayden saw a giant red-and-white paper dragon winding its way through the crowd. Hayden realized that the gunshots were only firecrackers. Chinese New Year. A banner held in the hands of children read YEAR OF THE TIGER. Two dozen Chinese dancers maneuvered the ceremonial dragon using sticks attached to its belly. Chasing the evil spirits away.

Hayden exhaled, laughing at his embarrassing display of caution. He stood and stepped absently into the street and collided with an eight-ton cable car and was sent flying.

About Stephen Jay Schwartz

Los Angeles Times bestselling author Stephen Jay Schwartz spent a number of years as the Director of Development for Wolfgang Petersen where he worked with writers, producers and studio executives to develop screenplays for production. Among the film projects he helped develop are "Air Force One," "Outbreak," "Bicentennial Man," "Mighty Joe Young," "Red Corner," and "Instinct."

His two novels, *Boulevard* and *Beat*, follow the dysfunctional journey of LAPD Robbery-Homicide detective Hayden Glass as he fights crime and corruption while struggling with his own sex-addiction. The series was recently optioned by Ben Silverman ("The Office," "Ugly Betty," "The Tudors") for his new media company, Electus, for development as a television series.

Stephen just finished writing "Grinder," a 3D action-thriller for HyperEmotive Films and Venture3D at Sony Studios. The film will be shot on location in Korea in the Spring of 2013. He has also written for the Discovery Channel and is currently writing his third novel, an FBI-based thriller. He lives in Southern California with his wife, two children, and a frumpy-looking labradoodle named Mollie.

Zoë Sharp

"Ill-tempered, aggressive and borderline psychotic, (Charlie) Fox is also compassionate, introspective and highly principled: arguably one of the most enigmatic—and coolest—heroines in contemporary genre fiction."

—Paul Goat Allen, *Chicago Tribune*

I'd give anything to have a character of mine described in the way Zoë Sharp's Charlie Fox, a former special-forces operative and present-day freelance lethal weapon, is described in the critical excerpt above. It's high praise and it implies the complexity of what Sharp achieves. If I were asked to characterize her writing in a single word, the one I'd choose would probably be "cool." In a world where lots of people act *cool, Zoë Sharp's books* are *cool.*

But as the review implies, they're not only cool. They're razor sharp, deeply felt, and heartbreakingly immediate. These are action thrillers about a woman who works as a bodyguard, frequently trying to protect women, and there's no cheapening the central issue of violence (often against women) as a means to an end. In fact, by wrapping this societal cancer in noirish, kickass, often funny thrillers, written in coolly polished prose, Sharp can take societal violence farther

Small ideas (theme) → build upon

and hit it harder than many so-called literary writers. And do it in language that's almost poetic in its economy and impact.

Zoë Sharp is one of the writers whose books I open with a bit of reluctance in case the new one isn't up to the earlier ones, because they're that good. And Fox's attitude is contagious. When a writer can get the New York Times to say, "The bloody bar fights are bloody brilliant," she's doing something very, very right.

The Simpler the Better

I like to start with a small idea—in some ways, the simpler the better. In the case of *Fifth Victim, Charlie Fox book nine,* the idea was this: "You don't know what you've got till it's gone."

I knew I wanted to approach this basic theme from two different directions. One would be the ongoing personal storyline of the main character, Charlie Fox. At the start of the book her lover, fellow bodyguard Sean Meyer, is in a three-month coma after being shot in the head at the end of the previous book. Charlie finds herself trapped in limbo alongside him, emotionally unable to let go, but finding it increasingly hard to hold onto hopes for his recovery.

To take her mind off this agonizing situation, I decided she would throw herself into her work. It's her job to put herself between her principal and danger, but maybe this time she would be that bit more willing to do so. She is filled with regrets over past misunderstandings with Sean, and fears she may never now be able to set them straight. At the same time the sympathy of her boss, close-protection agency owner Parker Armstrong, is growing into a stronger bond between them—if they let it. This would give me an underlying thread of conflict for the core characters during the quieter moments of the story.

For the plot itself, having set the previous book in California, I wanted to take Charlie to Long Island, the playground of New York's wealthy. I wanted to put her among a group of privileged offspring who have never wanted for anything and whose boredom with it all makes them careless of their own safety—until it seems they might lose everything.

I already had my title. At the start of the book there had been three kidnap victims. Another would be taken during the course of the story, and Charlie's task is to prevent her charge becoming the fifth victim.

To add to the conflict, I also knew that towards the end Charlie would get word that the man who put Sean in his coma was on the loose. She has the chance for vengeance—would she take it?

Those were my basic ideas for the book. The first thing I did was to write the jacket copy —as you'd find on the back of the paperback. This not only acts as a taster, but also keeps the direction of the story straight in my head.

Then I write the back-story of all the main players. I need to know why these people are behaving as they are, what they want, and what's driving them to get it. I jot down long rambling explanations for every significant character. And if they don't have much to do, I see if I can remove them.

At this point I don't have a plot—I have the motivations behind the plot.

Now is the time I usually have a bit of a panic attack because the whole thing looks a mess. I take to myPad (pencil and scrap paper) and make endless cryptic notes about every new development in the story, each time managing to progress it a little further, balancing the action with the reasons behind it. I was always the one in the James Bond movies going, "But how did the villain *know* Bond was going to be there in order to have a hundred identically-dressed henchmen standing by to attack him?"

I like to have the main structural highlights of the story firm in my head—the ambush, the double-cross, the revelation—but leave the reactions of the characters as a more organic process. By the time I reach that point I hope I'll know them well enough so they'll react in a realistic and believable manner. Nobody is ever straightforwardly good or evil and I love to play with preconceptions and shades of gray.

I wish I'd found a way to streamline the plotting process, but sadly I haven't. I need to keep writing it down, refining it, scribbling notes and then getting a fresh piece of paper and writing it down again. I've tried spreadsheets and index cards and computer programs— everybody has their own method.

My final outline is a POV one. I write a first-person narrative, therefore all action and information has to be channeled through Charlie's eyes—

nothing happens off-camera in real time. It's not simply a case of what's happening, but also how Charlie discovers each step of the story. I will often include notes to myself in brackets about who's doing what in the background.

A point about names. I jot down an alphabet and put marks above and below for each first and last name starting with those letters. It avoids confusing similarities and helps individualize the characters.

For *Fifth Victim* I offered a character name at a charity auction. The winning bid was from Dina Willner, who became Charlie's principal. Originally my idea was for a father and daughter, but Dina really wanted her late mother, Caroline to be included. It was a relatively easy adjustment, and she turned out to be great fun.

Being in charge of world-building for the book enables me to add in my own interests, like the fact Dina has horses. A minor point which — once included — becomes a vital part of the plot. I love it when something binds itself deeper into the story, making the whole thing stronger and more cohesive.

Finally, all my plots have 'E.&O.E.' at the bottom. (Errors & Omissions Excepted) Basically, this is the idea as it stands at the moment, but contents may shift in transit.

And they inevitably do...

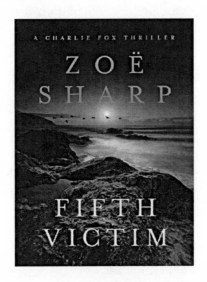

Excerpt

Fifth Victim
Charlie Fox book nine

by

Zoë Sharp

(Charlie is at the riding club with Dina and her horse, Cerdo. Dina has just finished a lesson from the club instructor, Raleigh. As they lead the horses towards their trailer, a masked man attacks Raleigh with a baseball bat…)

At that moment, a second figure emerged from behind another parked trailer, over to our right this time, and closed in on us from the other side.

His focus was completely on Dina, hardly even glancing in my direction until I moved to intercept. Then he tried to shoulder me aside with blatant disregard. To protect my hands, I hit him hard with an upswept elbow under his jaw. He dropped.

Cerdo had started to panic as soon as the attack began, skittering in a circle around Dina. Hampered by her injured leg, she could do little to stop him, although something made her refuse to jettison him. With more courage than sense, she clung to his lead rope with both hands even when he reared up to wave steel-shod front feet in her face.

It was a toss-up, at that moment, whether the greater threat to my principal came from our attackers, or from her own horse.

The man who'd clouted Raleigh, meanwhile, was standing over his writhing quarry with the bat still at the ready, as if he'd expected the downed instructor to put up more of a fight. It was only when Cerdo began his antics that he looked across and saw his partner on the ground. He twisted in my direction and stood there a moment, frozen, then hurdled Raleigh's legs and came for us with the bat upraised.

For a split second, time seemed to slow almost to a standstill, so I had time to analyze our situation with my options spread before me. All I had to do was choose. None of them looked good.

The parking area was out of direct sight of the yard itself. I could only hope that my own horse's sudden flight would bring people running, but how much use they'd be when they got here was another matter.

I gave momentary thought to reaching for my SIG, but dismissed the idea before it had formed. If I drew against a charging batsman at such close quarters, I'd have to fire to stop him. And not just shoot, but keep shooting until the threat was neutralized.

Instead, I chose the biggest and best weapon I had to hand.

Cerdo.

About Zoë Sharp

Zoë Sharp wrote her first novel when she was fifteen, and created the no-nonsense Charlie Fox after receiving death-threat letters as a photojournalist. Her work has been nominated for the Edgar, Anthony, Barry (twice), Benjamin Franklin, and Macavity Awards in the United States, as well as the CWA Short Story Dagger.

The series was optioned for TV by Twentieth Century Fox and one of her short stories has been turned into a short film. *Fifth Victim* inspired US singer/songwriter Beth Rudetsky to write and perform an original song— *The Victim Won't Be Me*. Zoë blogs regularly on her own website, www.ZoeSharp.com, and on the award-nominated group blog, www.Murderati.com. Find her on Facebook and on Twitter @AuthorZoeSharp

The Charlie Fox series in order: *Killer Instinct, Riot Act, Hard Knocks, First Drop, Road Kill, Second Shot, Third Strike, Fourth Day, Fifth Victim, Die Easy,* and *Fox Five*: a Charlie Fox short story collection

Jeffrey Siger

"This is international police procedural writing at its best."

—*Booklist*, starred review.

Jeffrey Siger lives on the paradisaical Aegean island of Mykonos. You might ask, "Why?" and I'll volunteer an answer: Because he can. He's one of the lucky ones who found his heaven on earth and had the guts to move to it. And write about it. Siger's alliteratively-titled books (the most recent is Target: Tinos*) demonstrate an intimate knowledge of Greece (both modern-day and ancient) and a natural writer's grasp of form, character, and story. His hero, Chief Inspector Andreas Kaldis, is an honest cop in a world of corruption and accommodation.*

Great stuff.

And as a plotter, Jeff is largely spontaneous, although as you'll see, he does make a list of bullet points—plot elements and other ideas—that lead him into the actual writing.

Plotting from Epiphanies

When I begin to write a book I always have a theme, but never a plot.

My themes arise from an epiphany-like moment of inspiration—the funeral of a close friend in a cramped Greek island church (*Murder in Mykonos*), the mention in a historical film of the ancient Athenian practice for ridding its city of unwanted leaders (*Assassins of Athens*), coffee shop talk among Greek friends of a financial scandal rocking an isolated 1500 year-old monastic community of twenty fairy-tale like monasteries (*Prey on Patmos*), or a casual remark about a jeweler's role in maintaining caches of hidden treasure amassed from the offerings of grateful pilgrims to an island known as the Lourdes of Greece (*Target: Tinos*).

Since I never know when to expect such a moment, I always carry a tiny notebook in my back pocket and a pen up front. I scribble down ideas, random thoughts, rarely anything more than a possible general direction to take the story. It's nothing remotely resembling an outline, nor as I've learned, close to how the book ultimately turns out.

All I have is this ethereal inspiration and, since I write a continuing series, an accomplished crew of primary characters chomping at the bit for me to give them something solid to work with.

So how do I come up with a plot? Damned if I know.

What I do know is that once inspiration strikes I immerse myself in researching the places, events, and entities I intend to fictionalize. I'm a big believer in predicating your story on accurate societal facts if you want to make the reader's jump to the unimaginable seem not that far.

And the more research I do the more "ideas" I scribble in that notebook. Then one day I read through my collected notes, come up with a thirty bullet-point or so ghost—not skeleton—of a plot, and begin to type.

I have no more specific idea of where I'm headed than does a fellow who one day decides to "Go West, Young Man." And though each day I may start out thinking I know where my writing is going, by the end of that session it generally bears no more resemblance to where I began than does a flower to its seed.

For some that may be an impossible way to write, but I can't think of any other way. Yes, there are points to cover, but how you tie them together is up to your imagination. There is no one right path to take. What drives you forward are instinct, glimpses of the Promised Land, and a Zen-like tenacity for overcoming inevitable obstacles. Some days it's an easy stroll across wide-open plains in soft summer breezes, others are a bare-knuckle struggle up a cliff face in an ice storm. But if you keep heading west, you'll find fresh, exciting characters along the way and plot shifts jumping out of trees. And every once in a while your characters might even trust you enough to let you write a bit of the story yourself.

But as with all good things there comes a time for the story to end, and the closer you come to concluding your novel the more control you must assert in plotting a course to the finish. A wandering plot is not a thing of beauty.

My practice is to make each chapter as perfect as I can before going on to the next. That means I've done a lot of rewriting along the way, and doing that forces me to envision more precisely where things are likely headed. I still often don't know what the conclusion will be until I've written it, but I can sense when there's one lurking up ahead just around the bend. The reader may not realize it, but I do. It's a moment determined by the pace of the story, not the plot.

No plot should stay beyond its time and if for some reason I think there remains something important to say that would advance the story, I go back into the book and find a place to say it there. Pace rules, at least in my book(s).

So, in a nutshell here is my ten-point approach to plotting:

—When the "big idea" strikes you, immediately stop whatever you're doing and write down everything that comes to mind, including where you see it taking you. Those first thoughts may later give you a plot you don't yet see.

—Imagine where you want the story to take place and immerse yourself in all you can about its past and present, especially quirky things. Take notes of every off-the-wall idea that comes to mind.

—Lock yourself alone in a room (key in your possession) with your notes, read through them thoughtfully, shut your eyes, take a deep breath, open those baby blues (or browns in my case), and start to write your novel.

—Your first few paragraphs can be important, for even though they rarely remain as you wrote them in the finished version, they can offer insight into where your book is headed. The first three paragraphs of the accompanying excerpt from *Target: Tinos* did just that for me.

—As you finish a chapter go back and rewrite it until you think it's as good as you can make it for now. It keeps you from forgetting from whence you came as you plot on.

—Do not be afraid to chase that random inspiration. You'll know soon enough if it's going to work and if it does, WOW. That feeling, my friends, is what the joy of writing is all about.

—Keep taking notes as new ideas come to mind and review all your notes regularly, especially when you feel lost. Consider them your map of otherwise uncharted territory.

—About a hundred pages into the book, try to hone in on where you think it's headed and aim to get there within the confines of how long your novel is to be. If you err, do so on the side of it being too long. It's always easier to cut.

—Read your notes again—have I said that enough times?— to be sure you've covered all that you still think essential for the telling of your tale.

—When the story is over, end it.

I apologize to those looking for a precise method to plotting. I obviously have none to offer. But for those freewheeling types who like to let it all hang out on a wild ride to an unpredictable finish, trusting only to their instincts, take comfort in the knowledge that you are not alone.

Excerpt

Target: Tinos

by

Jeffrey Siger

Revenge or Death.

That was all that the note said. It was found protected in a cylinder chained to the steering wheel of a van set on fire sometime before dawn. In the rear of the van was another surprise wrapped in chains: the remains of two bodies charred beyond recognition amid bits and pieces of an incinerated Greek flag.

"Freedom or Death" was Greece's national motto and by noon enraged network talking heads relentlessly decried the horror as a national sacrilege, with shouts of justice for the yet unidentified victims and merciless punishment for those "unwelcome foreign elements" tearing asunder the fabric of Greek culture with "their criminal ways." It did not matter that no one knew the truth.

"I'm sorry, but I can't make it," Andreas yelled into his cell phone over the whipping helicopter rotors.

"We must have a bad connection. I could swear I just heard you say you 'can't make it' to the only meeting I asked you to attend with our wedding planner." Lila's voice was in decidedly frosty counterpoint to the heavy, late morning air of July's last days.

Chief Inspector Andreas Kaldis, feared head of the Greek police's Special Crimes Division, cleared his throat as he said, "I thought you'd understand."

"You're a lucky guy," said Andreas's boss, Greece's minister of public order. "My wife would have killed me if I'd done something like that to her less than two weeks before our wedding." He smiled.

"There's still time." Andreas attempted to force a smile. Twenty minutes until they reached Tinos. "You do realize the press will be waiting for us?"

"It is their duty to report this massacre. We're talking about mass murder on the island of the Church of Panagia Evangelistria, the Lourdes of Greece."

Andreas could tell the minister was rehearsing his pitch for the cameras. Andreas preferred listening to the rotors.

Andreas stared at his minister. "Let's just try not to make any promises we can't keep."

By the late afternoon the facts, or rather the lack thereof, started rolling in. No identifiable footprints or other signs were found in the area, the van had been stolen that night from the port without a clue as to who did it, and forensics could not identify either victim. Neither the curious present at the scene nor snitches had anything to tell. There was not a lead to be found anywhere.

With Spiros having nothing left to feed the press, the media followed its natural instincts and began clamoring for his head.

Spiros had no idea what to do next. His limb seemed about sawed clear through and his career toasted to just this side of charcoal when two days later relatives of the victims stepped forward and identified the bodies: tsigani—known in other languages as gypsies or roma.

And with that the story seemed to fall off the face of the earth.

Lucky bastard, thought Andreas.

About Jeffrey Siger

The New York Times described Jeffrey Siger's novels as "thoughtful police procedurals set in picturesque but not untroubled Greek locales." *The Greek Press* said his work is "prophetic." *Eurocrime* called him a "very gifted American author...on a par with other American authors such as Joseph Wambaugh or Ed McBain," and the City of San Francisco awarded him its Certificate of Honor citing that his "acclaimed books have not only explored modern Greek society and its ancient roots but have inspired political change in Greece." *Target: Tinos*, the fourth novel in his Chief Inspector Andreas Kaldis series, was called "superb...a winner" by *Publishers Weekly* in a starred review, following up on his internationally best-selling *Murder in Mykonos, Assassins of Athens*, and *Prey on Patmos: An Aegean Prophecy*.

Born in Pittsburgh, Jeffrey practiced law at a major Wall Street law firm and established his own New York City law firm before giving it all up to live and write on the island of Mykonos. www.jeffreysiger.com

Yrsa Sigurðardóttir

"Stands comparison with the finest contemporary crime writing anywhere in the world."

—*Times (London) Literary Supplement*

Yrsa Sigurðardóttir writes dark, occasionally very funny novels set in her native Iceland, six of which feature lawyer Thora Gudmundsdóttir. With the burst in interest in Scandinavian crime fiction, it's taken some of us a little time to sort out the writers' voices (especially in translation), but Yrsa's is one of the most distinctive and addictive of them all. I've read two of her books (two more are waiting patiently), and neither of them would put me down until I was finished. Even then, their characters came back to me.

When you read her, it's easy to see why she's been translated into more than thirty languages. The narrative is brainy, muscular, pointed, funny, and (apparently) effortless, and from the first page the reader has that lulling sense of being in the hands of a writer who won't let him or her down. And despite what they say about no prophet being honored in his own land, Yrsa is winning awards right and left and right again, and has climbed to the top of the Icelandic bestseller lists as the rest of Scandinavia falls into line. And I doubt we'll be far behind.

musthave idea love the genre
look for storyline clues

A Craft That Can Be Fine-Tuned

A plot in this author's understanding is a series of interconnected actions carried out by the characters of a novel that create the spine of the story. If well-constructed it can be engaging, acting as the propeller that makes the reader want to keep turning the pages. If badly or unconvincingly done it can also act as the catalyst that causes the reader to put the book down once and for all, or even worse hurl it against the wall. Something no author strives for.

But how can a writer pursue the first and steer clear of the latter? Unfortunately there is no one brilliant method for this, as plotting is an art not a science. Although tips and tricks abound, it is ultimately up to the individual writer to find the tried and tested or unique and individual method that fits him or her to a tee. But even this does not make for the golden ticket as (to complicate matters) sometimes the same author will use varying methods for varying novels. What worked for the novel of yesterday might not for the draft novel of today. But despite this there is no need to despair. Art is after all a craft that can be fine-tuned by practicing and studying. The spark must be in place but stoking it can light the required fire.

Finding out what style or method of plotting suits you as a writer can be simplified somewhat by learning what others do. From this one can locate what is out of the question, if nothing else. Are you the writer that requires a detailed synopsis before putting down the first word in the novel or the gung-ho type that sits down and lets the story take the reins? This I cannot tell you, the answer lies within your own persona. What I can do is share some of the things that have helped me when outlining a novel, in the hope that something will come in useful.

Like any good storyteller I must begin at the beginning. The quintessential "where do you get your ideas from?" Without an idea for a book there is no book, just a white enticing screen that burns the eyes and singes the spirit. Therefore I never attempt to begin a novel without a clue as to what it will be about. Instead I begin by seeking the idea, purposefully checking my surroundings for the seedling. Sometimes it is a location, at others a news article and yet others a scene in a movie or words on the radio. What defines them as a whole is really nothing in particular, what makes them stand out is the fact that I am on the lookout. Focusing one's thoughts on the search for the next storyline. This is not to say that you never stumble across a storyline when not looking. This happens all the time but it helps to know that you have other options than waiting for the inspirational lightning bolt to strike your head. Work on it. Think about it. Constantly.

I am a firm believer that one cannot be a good author without loving and respecting the genre you write within. To love reading the type of books you write. If you are such a writer use this to your advantage. Spend some time wondering about what you would like to read about if you were seeking a book. This can work wonders. If completely stumped about the next novel, close your eyes and imagine yourself in a bookstore. Think hard about what text on the back cover would pique your curiosity. This can help you locate your seedling. Take it a step further and imagine the road you would like the story to take. Slow paced, full of surprises, creepy – what? Once you know this begin to think about how to achieve this. Keep going until you have the fundaments of what will become your next novel. Invite your brain to a movie within the confines of your skull. From this you can either write up a synopsis, as detailed as you feel comfortable with or simply start writing if this is better suited to your writing style.

This same method can be used when stumped mid-novel or within it. You have lined your pieces up but reach a point where everything seems to either drag on or stall. If you were the reader, what would you like to happen next? Never forget who is the navigator or puppet master in the world existing on your pages. It is you, the author. Whatever elements you need to make things work or become more interesting, you have them literally at your fingertips. Unlike the real world no one is going to interfere by doing something unexpected or cause events to go the opposite way you planned for. All you need to worry about is making the flow credible; if you need an airplane to come falling out of the sky just make sure you have underpinned the incident. If you realize that you need this to happen when you are well into the novel, go back and phase it in. No one writes by pen any more so fixing and tweaking is child's play. No fun at all, but thankfully doable.

When thinking out your story, never forget that if readers of crime fiction were only interested in crime they would simply read the papers. If the book is to be strong you need more than just riddle with a body. Weave something in that adds the extra depth making all the difference. Tie it loosely or tightly to your story of crime and the resulting read will be much more satisfying. Doing so is probably the easiest part of the whole plotting process. There is after all no limit to the injustice all around us and shedding a small light on one you feel strongly about or are interested in will not be a chore. Just make sure not to stand on a soapbox while at it. Do not become a dry pamphlet for a cause; the best way to avoid this is by moderating your stance. If you have a character that is anti-something, add one that is pro. This will allow your readers to draw their own conclusion and you can rest assured they will do so wisely.

Another thing not emphasized enough is using constructive criticism to your advantage. If someone you trust or your editor finds something wrong with the manuscript, take some time to ponder over what is found lacking or in too much abundance. If the people you ask to read over are trustworthy, they are not out to sabotage your work but help you. So listen to them and make judgment calls for each criticism, putting your ego to one side as you do this. Receiving criticism by e-mail beats reading the same in the review section of the paper, hands down every time.

Research is another important key element of plotting. Done right it will help avoid any unpleasant surprises that topple the house of cards that a draft novel usually is. Make sure you know what you are presenting and that you do not make any unwitting factual errors. It is bad enough to have to make the ones you do on purpose. This being the information age, getting material to read or view is easy enough although care should be taken when relying solely on the internet. This can be hazardous as facts presented there are not always as accurate as one would hope. Another issue to keep in mind is that you do not have to become the world's foremost expert in the subject you are touching on, and sometimes knowing too much about it is detrimental. If you have spent too much effort researching, you not only lose sight of what is generally known about the matter, but you are also in danger of information overload. You have invested a lot of time in bettering your understanding and want some returns. Keep in mind that if the reader wanted to read a text book on the matter, he or she would not have gone to the fiction section of the bookshop.

If your plot is to take place in a location you are not particularly familiar with, try as you can to visit this place and see it in 3-D. No photo or written word will provide the same sensory experience. When there note all things around you and imagine yourself as the characters struggling with whatever horror you have chosen to heap on them. Look for unusual things, check the dark corners and breathe in the essence of the landscape or cityscape. Many plotting ideas can come of this if you focus on using the backdrop for a purpose. Remember that a story without a backdrop will float a bit aimlessly in the reader's mind. You need a stage.

As I am assuming the writer I am aiming my words at is writing crime I cannot skate over a mention of the crime or crimes involved in the plot. Here it is of the utmost importance to figure out who is the villain, what did he or she do and last but not least, why did they do it. If you skip the last part you will not have much luck in making the story work as crime is usually committed for a reason. If you have an understanding of the motivation you will have less problems writing about the events that evolve around the act, or in some cases lead up to it. This will also help when peppering the text with indications of what is to come and keeping the reader guessing. If you really want to go the extra mile you add things and events along the way that you might not know how to solve while writing them. If you don't originally know how to work your way out of such a scene the reader will face the same question – "What the hell?" Put the writing aside and think your way out of it before going any further. There is always a solution. It is your world and you call the shots.

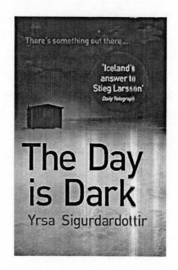

Excerpt

The Day is Dark

by

Yrsa Sigurðardóttir

Translated from Icelandic by Philip Roughton

Oddný Hildur turned off her computer and prepared to leave. She looked once more through the window and saw the dog still staring at her. It tilted its head, as if it were wondering why she had stood up. She regretted having given in to curiosity; now the dog knew that she was on her way out and would lie in wait for her at the door. However, it did not appear to be that cunning – it just sat there, still as stone. Oddný Hildur tugged at the curtain intending to block the dog's view, but when it emitted a howl she was so shaken that she left the curtain as it was and hurried out. This was getting ridiculous.

In the vestibule she put on a thick eiderdown jacket that had proven invaluable in this stormy place, and with the damaged face of the little girl in mind she took a scarf from one of the hooks and wound it tightly around her head, leaving only her eyes uncovered. Finally she put on mittens and pulled on the warmest boots she could find. Her shoes were wet, since she had once again forgotten to turn them upside down. The snow on them had melted as she worked, and made them soggy and cold. The same went for her hat, which had fallen off its hook onto the wet floor, so she also grabbed a fur hat belonging to someone else to keep the wind and cold out of her ears. No one would miss it, or the scarf and boots, if she came to work early enough the next day. She pushed her trouser bottoms into the boots and stood up stiffly. She was so warmly dressed that she could barely move, and it would be no easier when she got outside, with the wind in her face. She drew a deep breath and opened the front door.

Suddenly it struck her that perhaps the dog had been warning her, not menacing her – was there something else she should be afraid of?

The cold invigorated her and she pushed this thought aside. Her unease was probably all due to the video recording she'd just been puzzling over. Just before supper a clip had been e-mailed to her and her co-workers, showing the two drillers, mucking around in the smokers' room. Oddný Hildur didn't know who had shot the video; maybe they'd set up the camera themselves, since there were few others besides the two of them who could bear the little smoke-saturated room for any length of time. However, what had caught her attention was not their stupid antics, but something that shot past the window behind them without their realizing it. Since she had little interest in this kind of foolishness she hadn't opened the e-mail before supper, when she could have asked her colleagues about it. Maybe the apparition behind them was part of the joke? She had tried unsuccessfully to pause the clip and get a better view of it, but the movement was so swift that she never managed to stop it in the right place. It looked to her like a person wearing some kind of mask or strange headdress, and after it disappeared a red streak was left behind on the windowpane. The person – or whatever it was – had been holding something red, which must have bumped into the window or been dragged across it on purpose.

About Yrsa Sigurðardóttir

Yrsa Sigurðardóttir is an international bestselling crime writer from Iceland, the winner of three Icelandic crime awards for her work. Prior to writing crime for adults, Yrsa wrote children's books that landed her the Icelandic children's book award and the Ibby award. Yrsa has written 6 books in a series about her protagonist, the attorney Thora Gudmundsdóttir and her secretary from hell, Bella. Four have been translated to English and the fifth, *Someone to Watch Over Me*, is scheduled for publication this fall in the UK. English translations include *Last Rituals*, *My Soul to Take*, *Ashes to Dust*, and *The Day Is Dark*. Yrsa's recent standalone novel, *I Remember You*, has been nominated for the Scandinavian crime fiction prize, the Glass Key and is scheduled for publication in English in 2013. It is presently being adapted for the big screen.

The Thora series has been translated into over thirty languages and received great reviews world over. *The Boston Globe* noted it as being "Topnotch crime fiction" and "a facinating excursion into the macabre," while the *Independent of London* praised "the rivetingly gruesome inventiveness." *Publisher's Weekly* said that "Sigurðardóttir keeps the readers guessing," and the *Philadelphia Inquirer* that she "has the storytelling art down pat."

Yrsa works as a full time civil engineer in her native Iceland, writing crime fiction in her spare time. Amongst her recent engineering duties are the position of technical manager for mega project Kárahnjúkar hydroelectric power plant and project management of two geothermal power plants soon to be constructed in the north of Iceland. She juggles her professional carrier and that of her writing with her more earthbound family life as she is married with two children, one of whom made her a premature grandmother some six years ago. She lives with her family in Seltjarnarnes, overlooking the cold Atlantic Sea.

Kelli Stanley

"[Stanley's] prose sings with the cadences of early Hammett, middle Chandler, the outraged Walter Winchell and the young Herb Caen."

—Tom Nolan, *San Francisco Chronicle*

Not every writer invents a genre, but not every writer is Kelli Stanley. Similarly, not every writer can produce two series as different from each other as the ones Kelli writes. City of Dragons, *the "stunning first [novel]" (Publishers Weekly) in her Miranda Corbie series, recaptures the San Francisco of the 1940s in a way that evokes Hammett and went on to win the Macavity Award, a place on many Ten Best lists, and was a finalist for the Los Angeles Times Book Prize, the Shamus, and the Bruce Alexander Award. The second,* City of Secrets, *earned rave reviews and a Golden Nugget Award.*

"Roman Noir" came into existence with Kelli's Nox Dormienda, *set in the Roman-ruled Londinium of 83 AD, which manages to be simultaneously muscular, breakneck, and enlightening about a period of time I barely knew existed. It won (and richly deserved) the Bruce Alexander Historical Mystery Award. Here's how Kelli plots these firecrackers.*

Plotting

A Plot to Overthrow Writer's Block

Plot. Plotting.

Sounds an awful lot like plod and plodding, and when you're in the dreaded, soft middle of your manuscript, it can feel that way, too.

A plot, in common parlance, implies a premeditated scheme, an orchestration of future events... a forecast. Like real world plots, my plots take on dimensions that were not premeditated and that I did not foresee. Unlike real world plots, I can hit the delete button on any element that doesn't work.

So what constitutes a good plot and how does one create it? To begin with, you need two elements: an idea for a narrative and an idea of what genre in which you are writing.

Now, know in advance that I am not a genre box sort of writer... *Nox Dormienda*, my first book, combined the elements of historical mystery (1st century BCE Roman Britain) with hardboiled/noir style, thus inventing a subgenre *sui generis*. But if you're going to start writing a novel, it's best to have some idea as to what kind of crime fiction you're creating. If it's a thriller, pace (and action) are all-important. If it's a traditional mystery — and you have a series in mind — you'll want to spend plot points on character development and clue-setting. If you're tackling a police procedural, you can be detailed, perhaps a little slower, as the solution slowly unravels before the reader and your protagonist.

In the real world, of course, most good novels contain elements from multiple subgenres. My best known work, the Miranda Corbie series, lives first and foremost in the hardboiled private eye category, but is also a mystery-thriller-noir, with a *soupçon* of procedural and the detailed character development of a series.

Given these elements — and my belief that good crime fiction and good literary fiction are synonymous — *City of Dragons* and every other Miranda Corbie novel is built on a classical five act structure... which also influences the plot, as every act needs a focus and a climax, with the final denouement wrapping up multiple strands (usually three) of a plot point.

But I digress. We'll get back to structure in a minute. The second thing you need for a plot is an IDEA.

Keep in mind that it doesn't have to be fully formed… it just needs to be a hook, something to grab you and set your imagination free.

For example, *City of Dragons* began with one idea… I was researching Chinatown history (since I knew I wanted to set a book in San Francisco of the late 1930s/early 1940s), and I discovered the Rice Bowl Parties. These West Coast extravaganzas were held in Chinatowns up and down the West Coast during the Lunar New Year festival, usually over a period of three days and nights. Like Mardi Gras and Carnivale, they were wild, exciting free-for-alls, and brought hundreds of thousands of people into San Francisco's tiny Chinatown (we had the largest Rice Bowl Party on the coast). These forgotten city extravaganzas were held to raise money for China's defense against Japan in the Sino-Japanese War, and became obsolete when America entered World War II.

So, Rice Bowl Party was Idea One. Idea Two flowed from the same source material. In the course of my research, I discovered how many Japanese-American owned businesses operated in Chinatown at this time, how racism lumped all Asians together in a restricted melting pot, and how, in fact, the Chinese-Americans and Chinese Merchants Association had been urging boycotts of their Japanese Chinatown neighbors since the Japanese invasion of Manchuria in the early 1930s. And I thought to myself… how painful, how stressful, to be living in those few blocks of ancient apartment houses and crumbling brick, and to be at war with your neighbor, just as your homeland was at war with an aggressor. And what of the children who grew up there, side by side, Chinese, Japanese, Pilipino? As the song says, they'd have to be taught to hate. All of this real-life tension was rich material, and tremendously compelling to me.

Now, here is where the plot comes in: I combined Idea One and Idea Two. I thought to myself, "What if a young Japanese-American man—a teenager with a small-time record, someone whose death the authorities have little enough motivation to investigate—what if he's murdered during a Rice Bowl Party? What if my detective, Miranda Corbie, finds him? And what if the cops dismiss it as an example of the boy being the wrong race in the wrong place at the wrong time?" The excerpt below, snipped from chapter one of *City of Dragons*, will show you how this combination of ideas formed the nucleus—the hook—of the novel's plot.

I promised I'd mention structure. The Miranda Corbie books are built on five acts. When I conceive of a plot, or elements of a narrative, I not only try to figure out in which act something will occur, but I also draw diagrams and time lines to show the relationships between characters, the chronology, and motivations for the crime(s). I also decide where to put the mystery in mystery-thriller.

As a private eye writer, I don't have to concern myself with puzzles as much as, say, a traditional English drawing room mystery author. But I do like to surprise my readership (but not too much—you want a reader to gasp, and then to say, "But of course, that makes sense."). And as a series writer, I love to explore Miranda's back story, her history, and unravel it bit by bit in every book, while making sure the events and people she meets in one novel directly affect the next. I confess: I think of her as real.

So how do I keep track of all these myriad threads so that I can place them within my structure? An outline. Not an all-encompassing, everything but the dialog kind of outline, but more like a safety net and a road map to help me see ahead in the San Francisco fog. I know where the beats should go; I know I need to have a beginning, middle and end, and hopefully make my story and characters and chapters compelling enough to keep the reader turning the page.

At the same time, my outline isn't written in stone. Because I research while I write—and I write from beginning to end—I never know when I might find some odd bit of history that I want to use. Characters also take on a life of their own... some will even walk in and take over a scene. In short, I leave the fine-tuning of the plot to my actual sit-at-the-computer-composition, because discovery is my writing process. I can see a few things far ahead, but dimly.

All this may seem daunting, and completing a novel is no easy task. But if you persevere and start with a couple of ideas, the plot will work itself out—trust me. Story-telling is part of how we're wired as human beings, and as long as your imagination has caught at some filament, some hook, some narrative thread... you'll be plotting to overthrow writer's block in no time. Good luck and happy writing!

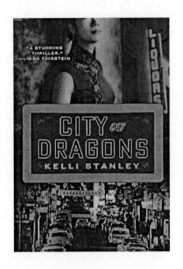

Excerpt

City of Dragons

by

Kelli Stanley

Miranda didn't hear the sound he made when his face hit the sidewalk. The firecrackers were too loud, punctuating the blaring Sousa band up Stockton. Red string snapped and danced from a corner of a chop suey house on Grant, puffs of grey smoke drifting over the crowd. No cry for help, no whimper.

Chinese New Year and the Rice Bowl Party, one big carnival, the City That Knows How to Have a Good Time choking Grant and Sacramento. Bush Street blocked, along with her way home to the apartment. Everybody not in an iron lung was drifting to Chinatown, some for the charity, most for the sideshow.

Help the Chinese fight Japan—put a dollar in the Rice Bowl, feed starving, war-torn China. Buy me a drink, sister, it's Chinese New Year. Don't remember who they're fighting, sister, they all look alike to me.

Somewhere above her a window opened, and a scratchy recording of I Can't Give You Anything But Love fought its way out. Miranda knelt down next to the boy. "You OK, kid?"

She guessed eighteen or nineteen, from the cheap but flashy clothes and the way his body had fallen, trying to protect itself. No response. She dropped her cigarette, and with effort turned him over, the feet around her finally making some room.

"Kid—kid, can you hear me?"

She bent closer. Couldn't hear a goddamn thing except Billie Holiday.

Nose was broken. So was his jaw. Missing teeth, both eyes black. What looked like burn marks on his cheek.

She loosened and unknotted the flimsy green tie around his neck. Eyelids fluttering, color gone, face empty of everything except memory. Unbuttoned the shiny brown jacket, saw the hole in his chest.

Miranda shouted over the music: "We need a doctor! Anybody a doctor? Anybody?"

The feet around her moved back a little, ripple of noise running through the crowd, music bright, singing about love. Always about love.

Couldn't risk looking up. His eyes were open now, brown clutching hers.

Love and happiness. Fucking happiness.

She took a deep breath and yelled, voice straining. "Doctor! Get a goddamn doctor!"

The cement was still damp with slop from the restaurants and tenements, and his fingers clawed it, looking for an answer.

The crowd shivered again, surged forward. His eyes asked the question and hers lied back.

"Who did this? Can you understand me? Who—"

He turned his head toward the direction he'd been thrown from. Last effort. Then the bubble. Then the gurgle. Then the cop.

"Move, you bastards. Move!"

His boots stood next to her, staring dumbly at the boy. "He drunk?"

The voice faded, happiness run out. The record made a clacking sound, and the needle hit the label over and over. Clack. Clack Clack.

She stood up, tired. "He's dead."

The record started up again.

I can't give you anything but love, baby…

About Kelli Stanley

Kelli Stanley is a multiple award-winning San Francisco novelist whose two mystery series focus on two fascinating historical periods and fictionally reinvent both. Her first Miranda Corbie novel, *City of Dragons*, set in 1940s San Francisco, earned the critical trifecta: three starred reviews from *Library Journal*, *Booklist* and *Publishers Weekly*, as well as winning places on all those "best of the year" lists. The second book in the series (and most recent to date), *City of Secrets*, also piled up the honors and was described by *Library Journal* as "neonoir in a classical five-act structure, starring one of crime's most arresting heroines." Her next Miranda Corbie novel is *City of Ghosts*, and Miranda is also featured in the short story "Children's Day," published in the bestselling International Thriller Writer's anthology *First Thrills*.

Stanley's second series set in Roman Britain, has also won numerous awards and honors. *Nox Dormienda* and *The Curse-Maker* are "Roman noir," and the City and County of San Francisco honored Stanley with a Certificate of Honor for her creation of the form.

Michael Stanley

"Impossible to put down, this immensely readable third entry from (Michael Stanley) delivers the goods. Kubu's painstaking detecting skills make him a sort of Hercule Poirot of the desert."

—*Library Journal* (Starred Review)

Good books of all kinds take us places we could never go on our own. In Death of the Mantis, *the guys who comprise the 2012 Edgar nominee Michael Stanley (Stan Trollip and Michael Sears) take us into a unique and fragile, but beautiful, world: the tragically compromised world of the Kalahari and its indigenous Bushmen.*

It's a world that balances deep beliefs, dreams, and secret, sacred sites against the unstoppable encroachment of the modern world and the innate failings of human nature, and those extremes are bridged in the enormously sympathetic person of Inspector Kubu (Kubu means "hippopotamus" in the local Setwana language) a kindly, if occasionally ferocious, cop operating in an environment in which far too many complex issues are forcibly reduced to black-and-white.

The subtitle of this series could be Going With the Wind. It's a sometimes melancholy and fading world, but here and there the human spirit shines out like a beacon.

inspired by events

When we started our first book—*A Carrion Death*—we didn't have much idea about anything. We had written lots of non-fiction—several books in Stanley's case and multiple mathematics papers in Michael's—but we'd never tried our hands at fiction. What we had was a premise. The premise had come to us in the Botswana bush after watching hyenas devour a young wildebeest. They ate everything except the horns and hooves. We speculated on what they would do to a human corpse. Nothing would be left. Nothing at all. What a wonderful way of getting rid of a body, we thought! Especially if you had a particular reason that the body should not under any circumstances be recognized.

Michael wrote the first chapter and sent it to Stanley. He was as intrigued and puzzled about the half eaten corpse found in the desert as were the ranger and scientist who found it. What happens next, he asked? Michael didn't have the faintest idea...

When Detective Kubu went out to the area to investigate, we still didn't know. We had lots of ideas, but we were coming to grips with all the issues around writing fiction. Who was it who said that fiction has to be believable, but biography doesn't suffer from that disadvantage? How right he (or she) was... We had been told to write about what we knew, so our plan was to have the scientist as hero. Fortunately, Kubu ignored us and took over, shouldered the academic and not too smart game ranger out of the limelight, and started investigating. He made one discovery after another, leaving a trail of dead plots in his wake. Somewhere a nasty family of rich and greedy people started to be the focus of his investigation. Somehow they started to fit the bill.

We can't imagine a more seat-of-the-pants approach than this. Kubu pulled us up by his bootstraps. Or is that our bootstraps? It was great fun! Maybe there was a freshness and excitement that came from the plot twisting and turning around us as it coalesced. When the dust had settled, a couple of reviewers commented that there was "too much plot", and they were probably right. Good thing they hadn't seen all the plots we rejected along the way! In the end, we were left with a plot with which we were comfortable, but also with a strong feeling that this was a very inefficient way to write a book.

When we started the second book, we were convinced that all this chaos was a spinoff of the fact that we knew nothing about writing fiction. It was only much later that we discovered that many mystery writers do it that way, enjoying the discovery of what's going on as much as the reader. By the second book, we thought we were experts. We knew better. We spent a lot of time plotting and arguing, rejecting ideas, following twists, taking turns. We had mind maps that couldn't fit on the dining room table. And eventually we had a plot that we felt held up and that would lead to none of the dead ends that had cost us thousands of discarded words in the first book. We sent our publisher an outline of *The Second Death of Goodluck Tinubu* and while a few extra embellishments occurred during writing as the characters developed and insisted on doing things their way, if you read that synopsis now, you would see that the final manuscript followed it closely. We felt we had cracked it! We understood how to write mystery novels. This must be how all the professionals do it!

Then came the third book, *Death of the Mantis*. We addressed it almost casually. We knew what to do. It was just a matter of enough work. For the first time, however, we found ourselves in heated arguments. Our ideas were quite different, and yet very much the same. This plot had no natural birth; like MacDuff it was "ripped untimely from its mother's womb." It wasn't for lack of effort. We actually spent more time on it than on the plot of the second book. Just as in *A Carrion Death*, the plot has suffered (rejoiced in?) major changes as we painted ourselves into corners or found our characters forced out of character. As we traveled around the world promoting *The Second Death of Goodluck Tinubu*, we argued about the plot of *Death of the Mantis*.

Our third book is a compromise between the two approaches. The first book was chaos, enjoyable chaos, and ultimately successful chaos – a true example of writing by the seat of your pants. Our second was planned and manicured. Successful too, we hope. An example of planning and careful execution. Our third was somewhere in between, and judging by the reaction, people think it's our best book to date.

And how about the fourth book – just finished a few days ago? Well, what we had was a premise…

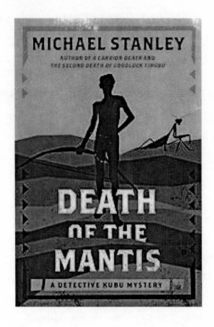

Excerpt

Death of the Mantis

by

Michael Stanley

The desert glowed in the dawn light. The Bushman boy woke from a deep sleep, still tired from the exertions of the last days. His father was already up, standing like a sentry, watching the sun creep above the horizon.

"We must go on, Gobiwasi," he said. "We will reach The Place today. We must travel while it is still cool. Here, chew on this as we go." He handed the boy a chunk of hoodia.

For the boy it had been a journey of heat, of sun, of exhaustion, as he tried day after day to keep up with his father. But he had offered no complaint, and now felt the thrill of discovery ahead. Today he would be at The Place! Very few people had ever seen it or even knew about it! He gathered up his few belongings, gnawed the root, and tried to match his father's easy pace.

After about an hour his father stopped and pointed silently ahead of them. Gobiwasi could see what looked like small hills on the horizon. He looked up at his father, and the man nodded. Then they set off again.

At last they came to the hills – a group of *koppies* rising out of the desert. They passed between them until they came to one in the center of the group - a solitary hill with a rocky cliff facing them to the east, steep slopes to the west. It was uniformly high north to south, showing caves and recesses from bottom to top in the cliff. They rested in the dappled shade of a scrubby acacia and ate and drank a little. Then Gobiwasi's father said it was time.

First they went to a large overhang in the center. There his father pointed out paintings of ancestors, men and women dancing, thin-legged, watched by gemsbok, eland, and springbok, gorgeous and strange representations that left the boy awed and a little afraid. Low down on the right, a lion, teeth unnaturally large, with a black mane and a long tail, seemed to growl at him.

Then they climbed to a cave many yards off the ground. The walls were black with soot, and on the floor lay a human skeleton, bones picked clean. Spread around it in a spiral were the contents of a hunting bag – spear, bow, delicate arrows, knife, cord, sandals that looked as if they would fall from the feet at the first step, leather-topped hollow root for holding the arrows, and several horns that Gobiwasi knew had contained poisons. To one side was a toy bow with small arrows – a child's precious possessions. And two necklaces of cocoons containing pieces of ostrich egg shell that rattled in dance. A Bushman's entire life lay on the floor. The boy wondered whose life.

About Michael Stanley

Michael Stanley is the pen name of Michael Sears and Stanley Trollip, longtime friends who in 2003 started writing mysteries together. Their books, set in Botswana, are police procedurals featuring Detective David Bengu, nicknamed Kubu. He is a large man with a love of food, and happily married to Joy.

Their first book—*A Carrion Death*—was published in 2008 by Harper Collins in the US and by Headline in the UK in 2009, and translated into French, Italian and German. It was nominated for a number of awards in the U.S. and was chosen by the *LA Times* as one of the top ten mysteries of 2008.

The Second Death of Goodluck Tinubu (*A Deadly Trade* in the U.K.) and their third novel, *Death of the Mantis*, were published in 2009 and 2011, respectively, by Harper Collins in the US and by Headline in the UK. *Death of the Mantis* was nominated for an Edgar, an Anthony, a Barry, and the Minnesota Book Award for genre fiction. It was also chosen by *Library Journal* as one of the top ten mysteries of 2011.

Michael's background is in mathematics and image processing, and he now works in Computer Science at the University of the Witwatersrand in Johannesburg. Stanley specialized in the use of computers in education. He has co-authored four published non-fiction books.

Their website is www.detectivekubu.com, and their Facebook fan page is at http://www.facebook.com/pages/Michael-Stanley/135421979876906

Solve it or Die
The Roundtable

After all the participating writers had submitted their essays, I gave the edited manuscript to about a dozen people, mostly aspiring novelists, to read and comment on. I asked them to come back to me with the questions they'd ask these 21 writers if they should meet face to face. Eight questions were mentioned more than four times, and I circulated those to the writers and received the replies that follow.

Certain themes emerge in answers to many of the questions. We all face daily the challenge of sitting down to the empty page, occasionally with empty minds, and finding our way back into our story. We all have to solve the thousand little challenges of making story: finding the idea, developing it, working with characters, events, pacing, tone, point of view, and on and on. And we have to sustain this activity—and the energy that propels it—from day to day, over a period of months or more. Writing a novel is the creative equivalent of running a marathon, and like a marathon it's done one foot, or one sentence, at a time, with the knowledge that the finish line may be a long, long way off.

Unlike a marathon, where once you start running, there isn't much to do except finish or quit, we have to push these daydreams along in the world of "real life," where absolutely everything can compete with the task at hand, and where—especially when we're having a hard time writing—it's easy to find other things to do. That issue is dealt with specifically in the question about the daily writing routine, but it's implied in the answers to almost all the questions, beginning with the first, where several writers stress that the idea they choose has to have the power to interest them for a long time. This issue—weaving sustained creative activity into daily life—is such an important one that we may do a separate book just about how writers deal with that challenge.

1. When you're weighing ideas for your next book, what kinds of things are you looking for?

MIKE ORENDUFF: I start with a philosophical question I want to explore. In *The Pot Thief Who Studied Einstein*, it was the role that chance plays in our lives. If you read that book now, you might see the question floating below the surface. But if you had read it before reading this, you would almost certainly not have seen it. It is not a plot device. It's not there to guide the reader; it's there to guide me. When I lose the thread of the story, I think about the question, and that helps me see the way forward.

REBECCA CANTRELL: I'm looking for something that will fascinate me, something I will want to explore for a good deal of my waking hours (and more of my sleeping hours than I'd care to admit).

For my Hannah Vogel books, I look for a pivotal moment in history that is rife with conflict and untold stories. In the latest one, *A City of Broken Glass*, I decided on *Kristallnacht* as the historical event I wanted Hannah to witness. I wanted her to walk the streets of Berlin on November 8, 1938 and feel the glass crunch under her shoes, see the smoke rising from the synagogues, watch the looters destroy stores, and sit inside a house while it was ransacked. I started there and worked back.

For the iMonsters books (*iDrakula, iFrankenstein,*) I look at classics and see which ones I can modernize and tell as a cell phone app. Not all classics lend themselves to that format, so I spend a lot of time reading and rereading books I love. Not a bad way to spend a few days.

For the Blood Gospel series that I write with James Rollins, we go back and forth a lot while trying to decide what would be fun and interesting for both of us. Since we're two people, more ideas come out and the books end up going in a direction I don't think either of us would have found on our own.

GAR ANTHONY HAYWOOD: I'm looking for the "hook"—that special twist on what may appear to be a familiar story that will make it uniquely mine. If I can't find that, no matter how much a premise intrigues me, I pass, because ultimately I'm always trying to write something that bears the mark of my particular perspective.

BRETT BATTLES: Generally, I'll have an idea of what the thrust of the story is about, and maybe where it will end. For instance, with the fourth of my Quinn series (he's a cleaner who removes bodies and makes crime scenes disappear), what occurred to me was a question: What if someone showed up on a security camera several years after they were supposedly terminated, and their body was disposed of by Quinn? It's simply a single sentence, but there's a lot that can be done with it. I might also (but not always) have an idea of how the book will end. Often, though, the ending will change drastically as I write.

JEREMY DUNS: I'm looking for ideas that will engage my interest and excitement for around a year of research and writing. More specifically, I'm usually looking for real events that took place during the Cold War that are intriguing and ideally not all that known about, which I think I might be able to weave a spy novel around. I also consider whether the ideas are commercially appealing and whether they've been done before to a significant extent. If they have, I'll probably abandon them—I quite often come across an event I think has possibilities only to find that several people have got there before me and used it. In which case I might kick a chair in frustration.

STEPHEN JAY SCHWARTZ: I usually have the opening scene in mind, so I'll throw that down on paper in outline form. I might have the first two or three scenes, and then it gets foggy. And then I'll have an idea for another scene, something that occurs later in the book. So, I jot that down after the first couple scenes, with a gap in between. Some scenes will be just interesting images or moments of vibrant dialogue, and I'll toss those in. After I have twelve or fifteen scenes, I break the page up into three acts and I determine which scenes are located in which acts. I usually don't begin this process until I can visualize the beginning and the end of the book. If I have the beginning and the end I know there's a way to tie them together, and that's where the individual scenes come into play – they become the guideposts for my evolving story. The hardest part is creating realistic transition scenes between each of the scenes I visualize. But, of course, all this changes along the way, and the scenes that motivated me to write the story in the first place disappear, to be replaced by scenes I might never have imagined at the start.

JEFFREY SIGER: To my way of thinking I come up with an idea for a new book when it starts beating me over the head. But a friend who knows my writing well and whom I respect immensely puts it more clinically. He says that I start out looking for a high-concept that is societal, historical, or in some other way REAL. One that intrigues or disturbs me and digs under my skin until I realize it's my next story. Perhaps he's right.

JEFFREY COHEN: If it's a new standalone or a new series, I'm hoping for a story idea that gets me excited, but mostly what I'm looking for is a character I think I can write convincingly who won't bore me to tears. If it's the next book in an ongoing series, I'm looking for something that will make the character face something about him/herself or just generally make their lives miserable, because stress is a necessary element.

KELLI STANLEY: For me, the narrative must offer something beyond escapist value. As a reader or movie goer, I look for an experience that will satisfy and challenge my intellect, engage my emotions, and encourage me to think about the story, characters and setting on multiple levels, both in terms of content and the style of writing. The more layers to the experience, the more you give the reader, the greater the book... whether it's "straight" fiction or crime fiction, the complexity of engagement is what defines literary quality and, in my opinion, makes a lasting contribution to the world.

ZOË SHARP: Something that will present an interesting set of questions for my characters—either physical or psychological; something that doesn't sound like same-old, same-old; something that challenges the reader's preconceptions; something intriguing enough to me personally that I will still retain a modicum of enthusiasm for it months down the line when I've wrestled the idea into book-form submission.

MEREDITH COLE: A great thing to ask yourself when you have a new idea is how much you love it. A novel idea has to be really enthralling and riveting for you before a reader ever gets to experience it. It's important to remember that you're going to spend literally years with the characters. Even if you're a phenomenally fast writer and get the book done in less than a year, once it's published, you'll be touring and talking about your book in the coming years. So make sure you have characters in your story that you want to hang out with, and a plot that keeps your interest. Please yourself first and you're sure to please other readers.

WENDY HORNSBY: Long before I begin writing, the germ of the story takes hold. That germ comes from ruminating about something I have encountered and that I want to explore. The Thing that drives the plot and defines the characters who populate the story can pop up anywhere, anytime. Usually, a story begins to build out of my reaction to something that has happened to me—or someone else—or that I ran across in the news, in conversation, from stumbling about in the world. It is the effect of that Thing that I want to explore physically, emotionally, intellectually. What is Its history and social milieu? Whose story is this to tell? The plot is the device that the story—the exploration—rides.

2. How much do you generally have when you actually sit down to write or outline, and what kind of material might it be?

JEFFREY COHEN: Material? You make me laugh. What I have is an idea of a premise, what screenwriters call a "midpoint," the moment (generally near the center of the story) where things take a turn that changes the character's perspective, and a very general idea of an ending. There might be the notion of a scene or two along the way but maybe not. Everything else will happen in the writing.

WENDY HORNSBY: When I begin to write I usually have amassed a hefty pile of notes, character sketches, photos of places the story will venture into, printouts from Internet searches, books that pertain, notes from experts I might have contacted, sticky notes with random notions, whole scenes and conversations among characters that I wrote and printed out. Once I begin to actually write, that untidy mass of research and prewriting sits, generally ignored, on the right side of my desk, because its work is finished. Almost everything that is useful to the story will organically find its correct place.

REBECCA CANTRELL: For the Hannah Vogel books, I usually have a great deal of historical information—personal accounts, diaries, letters, nonfiction books, photographs from the era.

For the iMonster books, I have the classic novel I'm adapting, a detailed outline of all the plot beats in the novel, and an outline of all the beats I want to bring into my story.

For the Blood Gospel books, we (James Rollins and I) have a World Bible with the basic background information on the characters and the stories (that is a lot of work to nail down, but worth it in the long run; I highly recommend it), a list of cool settings (this last book involved sitting on the couch with laptops saying "look at this!" and "we could blow that up!"), and some ideas of what the main characters will be doing and how they'll be changing in the course of the book.

ZOË SHARP: Ideas are everywhere—all you have to do is open your mind and let them in. Usually, I have a relatively simple premise, more of a theme than a plot, and from there the rest of the story develops. I have nonfiction books or articles on the subject, maps, and maybe even notes from visits, or a file with relevant bits of information highlighted, and the web addresses noted in case I need to go back again. Very easy to forget where you found that vital snippet. If anyone has provided me with research material or interviews, I note them as I go along in a file marked Acknowledgments, otherwise I might possibly forget to thank them by the time the book is done.

TIMOTHY HALLINAN: I generally have a situation and some characters and a setting. For *The Fear Artist*, I had the opening scene, where Poke is knocked down by a man who's then shot from a distance, and the cops deny that any shots were fired, and I knew it was the beginning of his becoming caught up in the War on Terror. Everything else came as I wrote, except for the old, unemployed spies to whom he turns for help. Writing series, as I do, there's a whole cast of primary and secondary characters waiting in the wings and hoping to hear a cue that will call them onto the page. This can be both a gift and a trial; while it's always fun to write characters I know, it's also exciting to discover new ones. But this time, the moment was right for the old spies. In addition to the basic situation, I'll also begin with three or four ideas for scenes and turning points, but I frequently dump some or all of them as the book comes into being.

3. Do your characters ever veer off the path you've envisioned for them, and what do you do about it?

LISA BRACKMANN: All the time. That's how they reveal themselves to me. So sometimes that means revising earlier material, in light of the revelations.

BILL CRIDER: Sure my characters veer off the path, mainly because I seldom have a plan. One example is from my book called *The Texas Capitol Murders*. In that one there was a character named Wayne the Wagger. He was a homeless guy who was supposed to appear in the opening scene while taking a whiz on a cannon outside the Texas capitol building, but I had so much fun writing the scene that I knew Wayne deserved a much bigger part in the story and that he wasn't just some random character I could write about and dismiss. I had to start the book over and make him a witness to the murder that sets off the whole story. And then there's Seepy Benton, who started out as a minor character in one series and who was so much fun to write about that I moved him to another series when the original one was canceled. He's still going strong though his original role has been long buried in out-of-print books.

TIMOTHY HALLINAN: Wayne the Wagger? Seepy Benton? How come I can't think of names like those?

WENDY HORNBY: Developing story characters is a lot like raising children. I can rein them in, do my best to keep them on task, but, if I've done my work well, given them proper foundation, they will have independent spirits and speak for themselves. I have planned for a character to be the perpetrator, only to discover that he/she simply was not morally capable of committing the crime the story is built around. At the same time, I learn that someone else is.

REBECCA CANTRELL: Yes, sometimes they do unexpected actions or reveal character details that I didn't know going in. I love that! Unless I'm pretty sure that the new information will drive the book in an unwanted direction, I usually follow the characters and see what they want to do.

Sometimes it's wrong and I have to throw it out, but often it leads me to a richer place for the story.

GAR ANTHONY HARWOOD: I don't actually believe in characters independently veering off the path I've chosen for them; I'm the boss in the stories I write and my characters pretty much do what I say without argument. But they do occasionally grow and develop in unexpected ways, and sometimes this has a significant effect on the course of the story I'm telling.

JEREMY DUNS: They do, and when that happens I try to look at whether their new direction is convincing, interesting, and can work in the context of the novel I want to write. Sometimes it doesn't work so I scratch it, sometimes I think it will work and so I pursue it, only to scratch it later, and sometimes I pursue it and it makes the novel better. I find that when I have a reasonable amount of text written unexpected sparks between plot points often fly, and they can make a big difference. A major plot point of my first novel didn't occur to me until I was about three quarters of the way through the first draft, and that was down to thinking through what my characters' motivations were.

ZOË SHARP: They don't so much veer off the path as get ideas above their station. Charlie's father, for example, a top orthopedic surgeon, appears in several of the books in a relatively minor role. Whenever he did so, he always stole the show. Eventually I knew he was going to have to be front and centre in a story. And some characters simply refuse to follow orders, so either I have to resort to blackmail, or frame somebody else.

KELLI STANLEY: All the time! And I *want* them to veer off the path. That's the discovery process in action, and a fundamental reason I don't obsessively outline. I trust my subconscious more than my conscious in terms of raw creation, and I don't want to inhibit it by confining characters to expected outcomes. I do, however, question developments that surprise me, asking myself whether this action is true to that character, time and place, and also whether or not it works within the framework of the novel. Should it be moved to another chapter or another section? What are the consequences for the rest of the novel if I allow the character his freedom? My advice is to let the character do what she likes as long as it works!

MIKE ORENDUFF: If I like where they're going, I give them free rein and roll with them. Their path is usually better than mine. The only free-lancing I prohibit is when they do something that seems to me out of character. They must grow as characters, but the growth must make them a fuller more complex person, not a new person.

4. What do you do when you get into real trouble?

JEFFREY COHEN: Readers of my work will find that the character, at some point in the story, takes stock of where everything is and what the character can do next. That's a sign that I've hit a wall and am trying to figure out where things will go next. It almost always works.

JEFFREY SIGER: I believe the only way to face terror is with confidence. Yes, you will have misgivings. After all, you're the idiot who got yourself into trouble in the first place. But, let's be real, folks, this is fiction. We can create whatever facts or characters we need to make it all work. Focus on where you want to end up and build an internally consistent, realistic, non-cliché bridge back to where you're stuck. That generally works for me. Cursing does, too, at times.

REBECCA CANTRELL: Curse and stomp. Then I go back to the outline, go back to the story, try to see where I lost the narrative thread. Sometimes I'll brainstorm ideas, such as, name ten things the character could do right now. I usually find my best answers at number 3 and number 9. I don't know why. But I've found giving myself the freedom to imagine many different scenarios (Hannah is abducted by aliens!) lets me see new possibilities.

I also keep a book journal where I whine and complain and think. I go there and do all that when I'm stuck.

GAR ANTHONY HARWOOD: I often try to charge headlong past it, and pay the consequences. What I do when I'm smart about it, however, is stop, admit I have a problem, and step back from the work long enough to sort things out, no matter how much re-writing or—God forbid—starting over is required.

WENDY HORNSBY: When I get into real trouble, I go back to the beginning of the book or story and start reading with a brutal eye. Usually if something has gone off track it's because of a flaw in the setup for the scene. Rereading, editing as I go, always reveals where the problem is.

BRETT BATTLES: Ugh. I hate when this happens, but it happen more often that I would like to admit. What I usually will do is stop, try to pinpoint the issue, then go back to the very beginning, and do a rewrite pass that incorporates changes the story needs to get me back on track. By the time I reach the point where I had to halt before, I'm more than ready to move onward. So far, this method hasn't failed me once.

ZOË SHARP: Keep Calm and Carry On. Seriously, a run out in the car usually clears my head— something that enables me to separate the whole left-side, right-side of the brain. I swear the practical half interferes with the creative half. Once I distract it with a menial task, I can usually make progress.

LISA BRACKMANN: Take a walk, or go to the gym. Or take a shower (I find showers weirdly inspiring). Do things that get my mind off the problem but that also allow me to work on the problem obliquely. I will also look to research for inspiration. I've found some amazing things that solved story problems that way, just surfing around or leafing through books. The thing about research is, sometimes you don't know what you need to know – so casting a wide net and seeing what's out there can be essential for how I plot.

The other thing I've found is that sometimes with a particularly tough project, you just have to hit bottom with it, surrender, before you can push the crap and the resistance away and figure out how to solve the problem.

JEREMY DUNS: I tend to go for a walk to clear my head, and perhaps leave the manuscript for a while until my brain has recharged and solutions start to emerge unbidden. I also sometimes dig back into research, either on the topic at hand or something else entirely. Watching TV also helps sometimes, especially if it's something totally unrelated to what I'm writing and not especially good! I just find that it opens my mind up to what I should be thinking about.

TIMOTHY HALLINAN: When I'm in real trouble, I do what I call writing about the book, as opposed to writing the book. What I mean is that I'll bring myself up to date, on the keyboard, about where the book is, and why I feel it's not working or can't find the next place for the story/characters to go.

Looking back four or five scenes (or story developments) and asking myself, "Why did I do this/why did this happen?" and often asking the corollary question, "What else could have happened?" It's best for me to do this at the keyboard because I'm only a keystroke away from being back in the story when the penny drops. When the penny doesn't drop, I bother my wife and tell her what the problem is. Almost always, she'll suggest something or ask a question that suggests something, or simply saying the problem out loud will suggest something. We don't always have to work in silence, you know.

STEPHEN JAY SCHWARTZ: When I get into real trouble I stop, re-evaluate, rework my outline and treatment and try to focus on the book's central themes. What are the major motifs? What is this book about, at its core? What is the through-line? How does my protagonist change? What does he learn in the end? Do I successfully map the arc of his changing character or have I buried it in muddled action or tangential subplot? Sometimes I have to step away from the manuscript for a few weeks to get some perspective. I get too close to it and I cannot form an unbiased opinion. When I return, the solutions to my problems usually reveal themselves.

BILL CRIDER: This is probably not what you want to hear, but I've never been in real trouble. Hard to believe that a guy who's a total pantser would say that, but it's true. I just keep on telling the story, and things seem to work themselves out. However, my favorite answer to this question came on a panel I moderated at a Bouchercon in Philadelphia some years ago. The incomparable Judy Greber (writing the Amanda Pepper mysteries as Gillian Roberts) said that once she'd written Amanda into a terrible mess and couldn't figure out how to save her. So she just said to Amanda, "Solve it or die." Amanda took over, and she must have solved it because the series continued right along.

5. *How do you decide what person the narrative should be in? What are the strengths and drawbacks of first- and third-person?*

ZOË SHARP: I originally tried writing my Charlie Fox series in third-person and she just didn't speak to me. Only when I swapped to first-person did I really find her voice. It does make plotting harder, though—I can only work with her POV, so once I've worked out a rough outline, I go back over it and produce a POV outline, making sure that all the information reaches her in a logical and believable way.

REBECCA CANTRELL: The Hannah Vogel books are all first person, which puts the reader right in her head and gives the books a stronger sense of immediacy. It also means that the reader only knows what Hannah knows, hears what she hears, and sees what she sees. This makes it hard to hide information from the reader or build up external tension by having the reader know something is going to happen before Hannah does.

The iMonster books are third person and, since they're all emails/web browsers/tweets/etc., I have to work extra hard to convey description and interior thoughts. It's like throwing out half of the writing toolbox before you start. It's challenging, and has forced me to grow as a writer. Painfully, sometimes.

The Blood Gospel books are third person, with multiple points of view. That gives us a bigger canvas to paint on and lets us do things with dramatic tension I can't with the Hannah books, but I also miss the up close and personal feeling of being in one character's head for the whole book.

I guess I'm saying there are tradeoffs no matter what point of view choices you make.

TIM HALLINAN: The great advantage of first-person is that it can provide you with a tone: it conveys a personality, an attitude, a point of view. It looks at the world and the other characters through one character's perspective, whereas third person, at least conventionally, is neutral: it presents the characters without making value judgments on them. (When I read a value judgment in third person—"He had all the personality of a floor lamp"—I always ask myself, "Who said that?") Being very comfortable in a character's first-person voice can make writing easier in some ways. On the other hand, third person allows us to follow multiple characters, to track things that are happening at the same time. That allows a writer to play with a whole new dynamic that can be used to great effect—that the reader knows things the characters don't.

MEREDITH COLE: Don't be afraid to try both when you're starting a new project. See how third- person and first-person fits the voice of your character by trying them on for size. First person usually feels more intimate. But third person clearly gives you more flexibility in terms of including other points of view.

WENDY HORNSBY: So far, all of my books have been first person, and all of my short stories have been in third person. The biggest drawback of first-person narration is that it limits the scope of the story, but at the same time it deepens the relationship between the narrator and events and between the narrator and the reader. It seems to me that the author's biases are bared more by first person than third, and those biases are an important part of the overall tone of the book; the majority of hard-boiled fiction is first-person.

6. What's your writing routine, and what do you do to hold yourself to it?

BILL CRIDER: There was a time, back when I was selling a lot more books than I am now, that I had a strict routine. Since I had a day job, I wrote in the evenings, starting at 7:00 P. M. My routine was simple. I had to write a certain number of pages a night. The count was variable, depending on deadlines, but the lowest ever was two pages. As soon as I finished the required number of pages, I could quit. When I started, I was writing on a typewriter, and two pages meant two pages, even if the sentence at the bottom of the page was incomplete. When I got a computer, I allowed myself to finish the sentence. How I held myself to this routine I have no idea. I didn't punish myself if I didn't get the pages done because I almost always did, day after day, seven days a week, 365 days a year. When I retired from the day job, I got much lazier. Let's not get into that.

BRETT BATTLES: For me, it's all about discipline. My goal is to write four to five books a year. To accomplish this I'm up everyday at 3:50 a.m., at my computer by 4:30, and actually writing by 5:15. My daily goal is 4,000 words. I don't always reach it, but do most days, and often surpass it. I write at about a rate of 1,000 words an hour, and with breaks, am usually done by noon. The afternoon is usually spent doing other things like promo, answering email, reading, etc. If I'm in edit mode, I'll start at the same time, but I'll usually go for up to ten, and on occasion, twelve hours. This helps me keep the continuity of the story clear in my head.

And when the book is done, I move straight on to the next one, spending three to five days fleshing out a concept I've probably already been mulling over for months, then diving into the writing again.

REBECCA CANTRELL: I drop my son at school and write until lunch. If I don't have my allotted pages for the day done, I don't get to eat until after I pick him up from school (2:30). He loves this because he gets to eat out on the way home from school. I hate it because I write the last 2 hours starving. Usually I get my pages done before lunch, which says too much about how motivated by food I must be.

ZOË SHARP: I write in the cracks of real life. For years I wrote around a full-time day job, and although I'm now lucky enough to be able to write full time, that doesn't mean I can actually sit at a keyboard twelve hours a day. I write notes for a chapter, then type them up, fleshing things out as I go. Then I have a break—cut the grass, take a walk, wash the car—and repeat the process. I try to write every day when I'm in the midst of a book, because it's so easy to lose momentum—not to mention losing the thread of the story. But as long as I do a decent number of words in a week I feel like I'm making progress and I can afford the occasional day off for good behavior.

JEFFREY SIGER.: When I'm writing a new novel I aim for one thousand finished words per day. At that rate it takes about three months to have a manuscript ready for an advanced level of rewriting. During those periods I try to confine my writing to between 11AM and 3PM—so to maintain some sort of "outside" life. But what inevitably happens is that as the book gets cooking I fall into a zone that has me writing twelve to sixteen hours a day, until my very understanding girlfriend slams shut the cover of my laptop.

And when I'm not at the actual writing stage for a new novel, I still write something creative every day, be it a blog or just comments to the blogs of others. It's like exercise. You must do some every day to stay in shape.

WENDY HORNSBY: I still have a day job, so time and energy are issues. I look at writing as a co-career and set aside time to write in the same way that my other employer claims a block of time. Having a deadline that comes with a check at the end is good motivation not to slack off, but I find that when the story is underway I'm usually eager to get back to it and feel a bit resentful that so much time is spent away from it.

7. What are the two or three best pieces of writing advice you've ever been given?

LISA BRACKMANN: Treat writing like a job – and the first rule of a job is, you show up, whether you're in the mood or not.

Establish a writing routine, and stick to it. The closer I come to writing every day, the more productive I am.

Learn to read critically—pay attention to how a book is put together, what works, and what doesn't, on the book's terms, not yours. Meaning, this is not about the book you would have written. It's about trying to evaluate the author's intentions and how successful she was in achieving them.

REBECCA CANTRELL: Julia Cameron in *The Artist's Way* talked about taking your writing as seriously as you would a "real job." She pointed out that you would never blow off work because the muse didn't come, because you had a headache, or because you didn't feel like it. You would go and put in the hours. As soon as I read that, I felt busted. I immediately started taking writing more seriously and the book I started that very week was my first published novel.

James Rollins always thinks about the reader, and says things like "Do you think if we do that we should just ship a razor blade with the book so the reader can slit their wrists after they get to the end?" Working with him has brought the reader into my head more while I write, and that's a good thing. For the record, I did change the razor blade version a bit.

For me, I also try hard to remember that it's always about me alone in a room with my characters—not publication, not awards, not even seeing the book in stores. Those are all cool, but it all starts and ends with me alone in a room with my characters and my story. So I try to honor and treasure that time and that relationship.

JEFFREY COHEN.: Larry Gelbart told me to "go where the pain is." I don't usually do that, but I think it's excellent advice.

WENDY HORNSBY: No question, the best piece of writing advice I have ever received is, Keep your bottom on the chair until the book is finished. How many people have drawers full of brilliant first chapters? Until there is a book, those chapters are meaningless.

The second, of course, is, Writing is rewriting.

If I may offer a third, I'll borrow from Somerset Maugham who said, There are three rules for writing a novel. Unfortunately, no one knows what they are. So, do whatever works for you.

BRETT BATTLES: First, read.

Second, a writer writes.

Third, it's all about the story, not about the method used to get to The End. Don't worry that you're not doing something right. There is no correct way to write a book, there are just different methods, and every writer's method is different. If someone tells you "this is the only way to do it," stop listening immediately. Your method will be your own, perhaps cobbled together from various sources or discovered all on your own. But that doesn't matter. It's the story. It's the story. It's the story.

STEPHEN JAY SCHWARTZ: I've been given lots of great advice, but the best is really the simplest: Finish the book.

ZOË SHARP: Not specifically given to me, but I still like Stephen King's famous advice to would-be authors: "Read, read, read. Write, write, write." You can't write a novel unless you've read enough to form an opinion—and read critically with an analytical eye. It's not enough to say "I enjoyed that book," or "I hated that book". If you want to be a writer yourself, you have to understand WHY.

Persistence is all. I firmly believe there are more persistent writers published than there are talented writers published.

Get On With It. I have this as my screensaver and it's always a useful reminder. If you wait for inspiration to strike, you'll never be published. There's no substitute for putting bum in chair and just WRITING.

And lastly (OK, I know that's four, but maths was never my strong point...) write what intrigues and enthuses you, not what you think will be a cynically commercial proposition. By the time the book is done you'll be sick of it if you didn't really love it to start with, and the latest fad may be something completely different anyway.

MIKE ORENDUFF: Rule 1: Don't agonize. Write a bad sentence that says what you want to say, and move on. Think of the bad sentence as a place holder. You can fix it later. Trying to get every sentence right as you go takes you out of the story. So your agony is doubled. You can't find the right sentence, and you aren't in the storytelling mode.

Rule 2: Re-write, re-write, re-write. When you get to one of those place-holders, the perfect sentence may spring to mind. If not, move on. It'll pop up the next time. Or during one of the scores of next times after the next time.

MEREDITH COLE: Just do it. Sit down and write every day. On your first draft, write as fast as you can and don't edit until your second draft.

8. What would be your personal advice for a writer who has come this far in this book?

KELLI STANLEY: Read carefully but don't feel constrained by other writers' techniques. Writing is a very personal process. Craft and various methodologies can be taught, but the best writing comes from the gut and the heart, as well as the mind. Ultimately, the best writing teacher is a great book... reading is learning. And write what you want to write, not what you think will sell!

WENDY HORNSBY: Know that all of us struggle, all the time. You write because something compels you, just keep at it. Also, find a couple of good critics—not your mother—and listen to what they have to say without arguing. The reader may be incorrect about why something doesn't work, but if it doesn't work, it just doesn't.

REBECCA CANTRELL: Love what you do. I'm not a member of the Dorothy Parker "I hate writing. I love having written" school. I love writing. I'm a compulsive writer. I wrote before they paid me to do it, and, should they ever stop, I'll still write.

Also, if you're unpublished, enjoy this time of writing what you like, how you like, and to your own schedule. Once you're published and have to start worrying about external deadlines, promotion, reviews, editors, agents, etc., it changes. Enjoy this stage as much as you can.

Finally, celebrate every single good thing. I celebrate finishing each major draft (to the point where my son says, "Didn't we already have ice cream three times because the book was done?), the publication of each book, good reviews, awards, good blurbs, a very good writing day, you name it. Writing has enough external downs, so it helps to celebrate the ups.

TIM HALLINAN: Don't let the Nozers get to you. The Nozers are the malicious spirits that have one simple function: to say no. No, this isn't good, No, you can't write a book, No, people won't like this. It amazes me that we engage ourselves in something as complex and ambitious as writing a book but we honor these snotty little voices who only know how to do one thing. I've named mine, and they're silly names, and I've gotten to the point when I can tell Stuffy from Pumpo and tell them, by name, to go to hell so I can just keep writing.

STEPHEN JAY SCHWARTZ: Read great authors and don't be afraid to let their styles influence your writing. Work to develop your own voice, but let the masters be your guide. Challenge yourself to write wholly original sentences. Don't let your work be defined by the cliches of others. Write every day, and read your work aloud. Develop an ear for crisp, realistic dialogue. Be a student of life, always.

ZOE SHARP: Build a complex story around a simple theme.

Don't front-load the back-story into the first couple of chapters-wait until the reader CARES about these people.

Every journey of a thousand miles starts with a single step. You can fit around three hundred words on a page. Write just one page a day and you'll have a decent-size novel in a year.

Even if you're a seat-of-the-pants kind of writer rather than a plotter, keep a summary of each chapter or scene as you finish it. Trust me, it will make edits SO much easier.

About the Editor

Editor Timothy Hallinan is the Edgar- and Macavity-nominated author of the Simeon Grist, Poke Rafferty, and Junior Bender series.

The twenty-one writers who have contributed to this collection have written more than 100 novels and have sold more than a million copies. They are Brett Battles, Cara Black, Lisa Brackmann, Rachel Brady, Rebecca Cantrell, Jeffrey Cohen, Meredith Cole, Bill Crider, Jeremy Duns, Leighton Gage, Gar Anthony Haywood, Wendy Hornsby, Debbi Mack, Mike Orenduff, Stephen Jay Schwartz, Zoë Sharp, Jeffrey Siger, Yrsa Sigurðardóttir, Kelli Stanley, and Michael Stanley

CPSIA information can be obtained
at www.ICGtesting.com
Printed in the USA
FFOW04n1421221113
2443FF